RONALD Golf Books by Champions——

Palmer: ARNOLD PALMER'S GOLF BOOK

Finsterwald-Robinson: FUNDAMENTALS OF GOLF

Casper-Collett: CHIPPING AND PUTTING

Littler-Collett: HOW TO MASTER THE IRONS

Berg-Cox: GOLF ILLUSTRATED

FUNDAMENTALS OF GOLF

DOW FINSTERWALD

WITH

Larry Robinson

NEW YORK WORLD-TELEGRAM AND SUN

THE RONALD PRESS COMPANY • NEW YORK

3

Library of Congress Catalog Card Number: 61-11067

PRINTED IN THE UNITED STATES OF AMERICA

Preface

It is quite fitting for Dow Finsterwald to put down in print the basic principles of the golf swing to instruct both beginners and average club golfers.

Dow Finsterwald typifies the basic principles of golf both as a player and as a high-ranking competitor on the tournament circuit. He isn't one of the longest hitters, or swashbuckling iron masters, or dead-eye marksmen with the pitching clubs.

He just plays with the calm precision of a fellow who knows his capacity and uses it with cool efficiency. He knows all the shots, as well as when and how to use them, and has a solid comprehension of the game that logically projects him as a ranking authority. Dow is the thinking man's type of golfer who has the keeness to understand what he needs to do to be a success in a ruggedly competitive business as well as how to acquire the ability to maintain his place at the very top of the profession with unflagging mastery.

The national Professional Golfers Association champion (in 1958) learned his golf in Athens, Ohio, where his father was a lawyer, a onetime Big Ten football official and a former football coach. Dow played golf as a student at Ohio University. Shortly after graduating in 1951, Dow decided to turn professional. In 1950, as an amateur, Dow had scored a 61 in the St. Louis Open, one of the lowest rounds ever scored by a simon-pure golfer.

Having served as an Air Force officer, Dow first hit the PGA circuit as a tour contender in 1955. After finishing out of the money in his first five starts, Finsterwald got going to end the year with official earnings of $15,386.96, not too bad for a 25-year-old who would still have been in law school if his Dad had had the say.

He moved up close to $30,000 the next year, and never since has he stood lower than fourth in annual total of earnings on the circuit. He has won the PGA, played on two Ryder Cup teams in 1957 and 1959, and won the Vardon Trophy in 1957. He holds the all-time mark of finishing in the money in 72 straight tournaments, a streak which ended at Baton Rouge in 1958.

Dow says his style of play is based on an honest appraisal of his abilities. Sometimes dubbed a conservative, Finsterwald admits the indictment if that is what it could be called.

"When I first joined the tour I decided the smartest thing for me to do would be to develop a swing that would keep the ball in play. I would rather have seven drives in the fairway and seven close than to hit twelve tee shots up the middle and be far out in the rough, and practically unplayable, with the other two," declares Dow.

"I weigh each shot in the light of conditions, always trying to keep percentage on my side. I try to get a mental picture of where I want the shot to go and what I want to do. I also strive constantly to develop my technique to do the job the way I want it done."

A young man thus gaited is bound to become a master practitioner of his art, well equipped to pass along the knowledge he has acquired by careful study of the manifold techniques which go into the make-up of a polished golfer. He has proved the value of conservatism and normalcy in a game which requires intelligent perseverance to become a finished player. You will not be given any trick ways of playing golf by Dow Finsterwald. He advocates, and propounds, a sound approach and orthodox training procedure, the best foundation for the improvement of one's game and a guarantee of greater future enjoyment of a grand pastime to those who heed his counsel.

Larry Robinson

Flushing, New York
February, 1961

basics
to a

Contents

FUNDAMENTALS OF GOLF

1

Briefing the Beginner

Golf is not too difficult a game to learn. Not that a rank beginner can merely pick up a club and start playing well. He will be lucky if he can hit the ball the first few times he tries. But with a few swings, and some advice on adjustments, he will get the idea and some appreciation of the game.

Remember that no game can be played expertly at the very outset. To achieve confidence the novice must take time and devote some effort before he can step up to home plate, swing a hockey or lacrosse stick, bowl, or take part in any of the other pastimes requiring some physical skill. Golf, with its long-distance results on the fairways and its oft-demanded delicacy on the greens, requires special effort and attention on the part of the beginner.

Perhaps the greatest handicap a beginner faces in golf is experience with baseball as a child. That extends to the women, too. It is a rare youngster of either sex, indeed, who has not played baseball and swung at a thrown ball across home plate.

Both are swings, but there is complete dissimilarity between a baseball swing and that of golf. At home plate, the batter uses a palm grip and a swing at or about waist height. Considerable adaptation of the swing is necessary to convert to the action of a good swing with any golf club.

In baseball the batter must pick off, in mid-air, a moving ball thrown by someone who is more than reluctant to have the ball hit. Yet I say that the baseball swing is much simpler and easier to master. For one thing, it involves less complexity of muscular action and certainly far less coiling and uncoiling of the arms, legs, and torso through different planes.

In acquiring certain basic principles of the golf swing, there is a certain elementary procedure which everyone must observe. This is what I hope to impart to the reader, using as simple and understandable terms as possible. I know I will sometimes employ words and phrases which are strictly the lingo of golf, but the game has become so widespread in America today that I feel almost everyone will understand what I write.

DEVELOP YOUR OWN POTENTIAL

This I would like to impress on every reader: in the first stages of learning to play golf, the main objective should be to develop a technique which will assure clubhead speed at impact—under full control. Forget any ideas of coming up with the so-called perfect swing. Just try to develop your own full potential by careful observance of proven methods.

That is an extremely important point to remember. It just isn't possible for anyone to prescribe a perfect swing, or to achieve it if someone could lay down such a formula. I have found, along with most of my associates in professional competition, that a golf swing is a personal thing. Each player's swing is different from anyone else's, even though the variation is recognizable only to the expert eye.

For example, suppose you felt that you would be able to master the art of playing good golf by duplicating exactly the style of your own club champion, let us say, or of any other outstanding player who may have caught your fancy. Granted that your chosen model boasts all the components of a good swing—smoothness, even tempo, plenty of power, and a good touch. You can copy his standard actions of stance, timing, and so on; but there is no way whereby you can swing exactly as he does. Never forget for a moment that each player has his own personal swing, one which cannot possibly be duplicated precisely by anyone else.

Even two players with exactly the same build and body conformations will have different swings, and this includes twins. The reason is not hard to understand. It involves muscular development, visual perceptiveness, coordination of nerve control, leg muscles, and on and on. No two men have exactly the same strength of wrist or fingers or the same development of extensor muscles; nor, if they do, would they have the same instinct for timing or weight balance. Any one of these factors means that no one can exactly duplicate another no matter how closely he comes to a perfect imitation. Anyway, if an individual has the ability to come close to following the technique of his model, he undoubtedly would do much better to develop his own potential.

You do not need the build of a rangy end or a big-muscled fullback to develop a good game. Little fellows can stand with giants for distance off the tee. You have an advantage if you recognize this fact at the very outset. Within yourself lies a potential which only you can develop. Competent advice will help to speed up the job, and that is what I hope to give my readers.

A good golf game cannot come completely from printed pages because it requires too much active work on the part of the player, plus a great deal of repetition and trial-and-error procedure. But if the beginner will give intelligent attention to certain basic principles which are set down within these covers, he has a far greater chance of bringing his game to a quicker, more satisfying stage on the path to be coming a good golfer.

The greatest reward you can get out of golf is the pure enjoyment of a fascinating, unpredictable game. It requires a technique which will never be completely mastered by any human. The more you learn about it, the more you will realize its endless variations and the more absorbing it will become to you. You will find that even the bad moments have interesting overtones, though they may become enjoyable only in long retrospect.

Throughout your experience with golf, from being a rank novice to becoming an experienced par-buster if you are so lucky, you seek to acquire and retain a swing action which will become as nearly automatic as possible. You have become a top golfer when you can step up to the ball and hit it approximately the distance and direction you desire, without giving a preliminary thought to the techniques involved.

This means that you have developed certain habits involving the various components of a swing—grip, stance, address, swing, timing, follow-through, and what not—which have become built-in, automatic reflexes. When this happens, you have found the coordination which makes for good scoring via good control.

CONCENTRATE ON FUNDAMENTALS

If you are a beginner, try to stay away from everything but acquiring the fundamental theories and proper use of grip, stance, and swing. All the intricate and often unfathomable refinements attached to a golf swing, so freely cited by the experts, should be saved for the day when you feel you are playing satisfactorily and with some regularity.

The advanced techniques will be just as much a plague to you then, but by that time you will have the ability to adapt some of the formulas, mainly by the trial-and-error method. There is no hard-and-fast formula for anything in golf except the score you have made after you hole out. Even the rules require extensive interpretation by a committee of experts from the top drawer of the United States Golf Association, the final authority on the playing of the game in this country.

At this point, I must impress upon prospective golfers the value of knowing the rules. I say that a complete knowledge of the code is an absolute essential in the process of learning golf. The Rules of Golf will not teach you how to swing at the ball or correct a bad slice. But a careful reading of the complete code, and a little personal prying into the reasons, will help you tremendously in the art of playing the game.

Bear in mind that mainly you are trying to develop a game which you will enjoy playing because of the better results you get from your efforts. I can lay down basic principles and advise you on correct procedure, but in the end, the game you play must be your own personal production. As you make some progress in the early stages, always bear this important fact in mind.

Your real aim should be to get your game in good enough shape to "get away with it." As I said before, it is impossible to acquire a perfect game, or ever to master the art of golf completely.

Now you may not be the best swinger on the course, or even in your own four-ball group. But if you bend every effort to doing well with the ability you have, you will get a lot more mileage than the fellow who just bangs away—a fact of the game which has been proved time and again. I say this with my own game in mind, as well as that of many of my contemporaries. Golf is a game of near misses, and the principal aim always should be to bear down hard on keeping the errors to an absolute minimum.

Time and again I have seen players who admittedly are not the best in the field (and include me among them) win major tournaments and championships because they avoid trouble by good thinking, careful planning, and fine nerve control. The idea is to get maximum advantage by utilizing every bit of one's talents, avoiding the bad mistake. Don't ever let conditions such as a big, tough course, or a high wind, or unfamiliar turf cause you to lose your poise, which inevitably leads to forgetting fundamentals so painfully acquired.

There is as much fascination in good manipulating as in sinking a long putt. Constantly in your golfing career you will be called on to hit shots you know are not your strong point. If you learn how to manage your game in these situations, you are well on the way to becoming a solid player.

That is what makes golf the best of all games, to my mind. There is wonderful exhilaration in hitting a long, straight drive or a well-placed approach or in sinking a long, curling putt. And I have found just as much thrill in a fine recovery, or earning a par where it seemed to need a miracle to get a bogey, as in racking up a low total score.

A good game of golf takes good swinging and, even more, good thinking. I admit, in making this statement, that the swing must come first. If you don't know the rudiments of hitting the ball and the proper technique, all the good thinking in the game is not going to produce even the remote semblance of a good shot.

SAVE THE REFINEMENTS FOR LATER

The beginner, therefore, should concentrate on acquiring a sound swing procedure in the early stages. He probably will have to listen to a lot of technical talk and discussion of shot-making and par-saving methods, to his early confusion. But pay no attention to such shop talk at first. It will become more understandable and available as one's technique improves;

or maybe I should say that it will naturally follow as the player becomes more indoctrinated.

I know this was true in my own case. When I first took up golf, I must admit I was not overly enthusiastic about it. It was just something to do for a thirteen-year-old who had a summer job in the locker room at the Athens Country Club in Ohio where my dad was a member but not a very good player. My duties afforded me considerable opportunity to play, and I took advantage of it. I did not have any instruction, or any desire for it.

My start as a golfer is one of the reasons why I do not think a beginner should try to heed all of the theories of swinging which will be offered him gratis on every side from individuals who have no firm basis for giving such advice. I just learned to hit the ball without benefit of advice. At the outset I used the regular baseball grip (placing each hand independently of the other on the grip) because it was the only way I knew.

Later in the summer one of the members told me about the Vardon, or overlapping, grip and gave me a demonstration. With a typical youngster's curiosity I tried it. Eventually I adopted it as a permanent part of my game, but without any conviction at first.

Actually, I don't subscribe to any invariable preference of one grip over another. I would leave the choice to the player—after he has learned the rudiments of the game and can do some thinking on his own about his game.

The grip which feels best, or gets the better results, is the one to adopt. It is said that the Vardon grip brings the hands closer together to work more in unison and therefore may be preferable to a beginner since that makes it something of a short cut on the way to learning techniques.

I find myself varying my hand position on the shaft from day to day, although I always use the overlap grip. It all depends on how my hands feel on that particular day before I tee off, or even midway in a round. If they are "thin," as the pros say of a player who finds himself hitting with unexpectedly good form, then I might be a bit bolder in my gripping than on a round when the club feels more like a baseball bat in my hands, which to me means no feeling at all.

Here, however, is part of the refinement of technique that comes with more knowledge of the golf swing, which only can be gained by experience. The novice need fret over no such problem. I mention it merely to illustrate a future point to consider. It also lets you realize there can be leeway in such matters.

Don't ever forget that whatever swing you develop, it is going to be yours as long as you play golf. You can and will tinker with grip, stance, and weight shift, and all the other variations which have been advanced by sundry experts for a hundred years and more.

But these will effect little or no alteration of your fundamental swing action. Therefore it behooves the beginner to get started in the sound, orthodox way. If he can develop an easy, smooth action at the outset, it will remain as long as he plays the game.

Only on rare occasions have golfers been able to discard or eliminate their old swings and substitute a new and different one. I hate to think of the tedious routine which the few who did this were forced into to accomplish the drastic change. Furthermore, I don't believe it was worth the effort.

OVERCOMING TENSION

There are many factors pertaining to golf which cannot be covered in a book. One, in particular, is muscular and nervous tension. As a teacher, all that one can do is to draw attention to its existence and advise against any tendency to get overwrought.

Much of this hinges on the make-up of the individual player. Some people are naturally hypertense; others might even need to crank up their nerves when they step on the tee to be fully efficient. A more placid nature might react productively to a situation which would shatter a nervous type.

Each player must eventually work out his own nerve control by ascertaining just where his breaking point may be. On the pro tour some of the players are the high-tension type and suffer because of it. They must constantly battle the tendency to grip too tightly, stand too rigidly, or commit other faults which ruin a shot.

The experienced player has discovered various ways of combating such threats. Some key their perception of potential errors-to-come on an overtaut feeling in their hands and wrists, or perhaps an unusual stiffness of knees or legs. Others may sense it by unusual constriction of the shoulders or of the entire body.

Naturally the best place to overcome it is in the mind, but there are numerous physical ways to compensate as well. Some use the wiggle and waggle during address to overcome tautness. Others talk themselves out of it. Still others will employ the so-called "forward press," a slight forward movement of the hands just before starting the backswing. Any gimmick which can relieve tightening of the swing should be used; and it is the player himself who must determine the most effective measure.

These are things which can be advised but not taught. The player is his own teacher here and therefore must work out his own salvation and countermeasures.

PRACTICE

As you progress in learning golf, there is the matter of practice procedure to consider. A majority of average golfers who go out for an occasional drill session will spend most of the time hitting the clubs they use the best. They get esthetic enjoyment out of watching the good shots fly away.

But a touring pro never works on the "good" clubs. He concentrates on the one he was hitting badly the last time he was on the course, or on the ones he feels he has never gotten under full control.

Never practice just to hit shots!

Go out to improve your shortcomings and stick to your purpose. There is no chance whatever of improving by merely batting a lot of balls off the practice tee. You must have an objective to profit from such sessions— with one exception. That is the brief warm-up just before teeing off on any round.

The latter procedure is one I would make a must in everyone's playing routine. Every good player observes this ritual conscientiously. Few club members ever do it. I will never understand why they pass up this chance to save at least five strokes with only a few minutes of extra effort.

As I write this, the most frequent complaint of teaching pros—and I have suffered the same experience myself—comes to mind. It is the tendency of pupils to take a lesson or a series of lessons and apparently gain something of value from them. They go out for a round with their friends, or friendly enemies, and either completely forget all that they have been told, or revert to their old method after a couple of tries with the technique the pro advised because the shot failed to come off as well as it did on the teaching tee.

It is easy to forget some of the advice given by your pro, I will admit. It is even difficult at times and under stress to recall something you may have worked out by yourself in a practice session. But a player who wants to improve should make a determined effort to remember why he had been hitting bad shots and the basic counsel of the expert to whom he turned for help. Believe me, the golf pro knows what he is talking about.

I think I was most fortunate in my development as a golfer to have had a fairly orthodox style of playing. That may sound like boasting, and perhaps it is; but actually I mean to say that I take the club back and down in a reasonably consistent pattern. It is far from perfect, as I unwittingly demonstrate in tournaments on numerous occasions and not of my own volition. But it gets the job done. And this brings us back to my previous point of getting the utmost value of the material at hand—in this case, your own swing. That should be the aim of every neophyte.

The first problem, of course, is the matter of hitting the ball squarely, getting the club in at the point of impact with a solid blow. Once having adjusted oneself to hitting a ball with some degree of accuracy, all effort then should turn to acquiring a smooth, constant acceleration of backswing and downswing, particularly the latter.

Make sure the clubhead travels in as true a path as possible both up and down, with no jerks or hitches because of faulty grip or stance.

This I know: the better you play golf, the more you will play it. A striking example of this is the professional who pursues the long tournament circuit from one side of the country to the other, winter and summer. Here is a fellow who plays four rigidly prescribed rounds each week under full tournament conditions, and practices intensively on the other three days. It is not easy with tonight's lodging and tomorrow's meals and Monday's trip to the next championship to arrange and with the funds perhaps depending on how well he plays today. One bad shot can wipe out this week's salary.

Yet where do you find these same pressurized competitors when they have some time to themselves? On the golf course! Even though it is their sometimes arduous vocation, they love the game and the infinite variety of its play. The same course can play four different ways on four successive days.

These top stars seldom hit what they consider a perfect shot, either, even though it may look as though they do to the average club player. But they are always trying, and enjoy doing it. So will you. Particularly if you start right!

2

The Grip

The man or woman just taking up golf enjoys an advantage which he does not appreciate until he has delved more into the myriad aspects of the game. He is under no necessity to revamp his game to eliminate faults, because he hasn't acquired any as yet. Starting from scratch, the beginner has the chance to develop a correct, orthodox swing.

Therefore, if the beginner will apply himself to observe certain fundamental principles in regard to grip, stance, and swing—the three basic divisions of the art of hitting a golf ball—he will have given himself a good opportunity for a pleasurable future in a wonderful game.

At the outset of his introduction to the game, a player may have trouble even hitting the ball, or getting it off the ground. However, it does not take too much time or too much practice to overcome the strange feeling of hitting a motionless little white ball off the ground and of getting loft from the pitch of the face of the club.

Once the player has the idea of getting the ball up in the air—of getting loft from the pitch of the face of the club—he has passed the crucial test, no matter what distance he may hit the ball.

THE IMPORTANCE OF A GOOD GRIP

Many experts teachers flatly declare that the entire golf swing hinges on a correct grip. They hold that if the club is held in the hands properly, then everything else will follow through naturally. I cannot admit that I am in complete accord with this all-encompassing claim. But, on the other hand, I do not want to minimize in the least the importance of a good hold on the club.

It is important for you to keep in mind the fact that your golf grip must be different from the way you would take hold of a bat. The golf ball lies down at your feet, for one thing, which requires some physical adjustment in relation to holding a baseball bat, let's say. The way you hold a golf club, therefore, can be considered somewhat alien to your experience with any other club, even a hockey stick.

Your golf grip is taken first to insure a proper hold on the club, and

Fig. 1.   The No. 5 iron, basic club of the irons.

secondly to make sure it will not be affected by the violent effort of taking the club back and then literally wrenching your arms down in the same path. You must hold the club, too, so that it will not deviate too much from the line of the backswing and the downswing throughout its entire route. To insure this, certain tested rules of gripping must be followed.

At first the orthodox golf grip might feel a bit uncomfortable. But bear in mind that within a short time, it will feel much more usable. Eventually, as your play develops, you will understand the reason for the prescription.

The orthodox grip can be used by everyone with two arms and hands, regardless of physique, physical strength, or size of the hands. The fellow with the big strong hands, of course, will have an easier time of it. But golf is no more rewarding to the ham-handed than to the smaller-boned person if the latter makes certain he starts the game using the correct technique.

For purposes of standardization I have a No. 5 iron in mind as the starting club for my pupil to use. (See Fig. 1.) It could be any one of several other irons, since all are gripped similarly except for the special shots, such as a choked pitch. This is not the time to go into these shot-making refinements, which require considerable experience and some inside knowledge to master.

I pick the No. 5 iron because it is midway in loft of all the iron clubs in your bag. It is also the dividing club between the pitching weapons, which are deep-faced, and the long-distance irons with their narrower faces and steeper pitch.

TAKING THE GRIP

Before taking the club in hand do this: face the hands against each other at waist level, with palms open about four inches apart. Make sure that they are in complete opposition to each other. This is exactly the way they still should be when you take hold of the club, but with the fingers properly placed on the leather grip, of course. (See Fig. 2.) If they are not in opposition, then you will be prone to develop the common fault of letting one hand dominate the other. Guard against this fault by every means within your power.

You can start taking the grip by placing either the left or the right hand on the shaft first, whichever feels natural to you. The hand placed first on the shaft then becomes a guide for the other. Personally, I prefer to put the left hand on the club first, and for two logical reasons. Since you are going to take either the overlapping, the interlocking, or the unlap grip, the left hand affords a more natural progression in placing the little finger of the right hand. Also, it is easier to check your hold with both hands to make sure that the hands are exactly opposite.

First, with a loose and non-method grip, place the face of the club behind the ball, which should be about midway between the toes and the natural club-length distance away. Be careful that you need neither reach out to hit the ball nor cramp your downswing by standing too close. Center the clubface behind the ball.

Fig. 2.   The position of the hands, opened before taking the grip.   The palms are in opposition to each other.

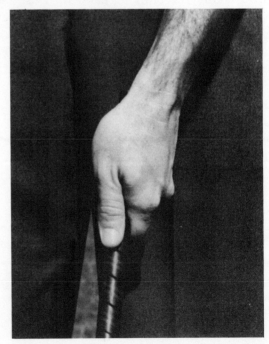

Fig. 3.   A solid position of the left hand.

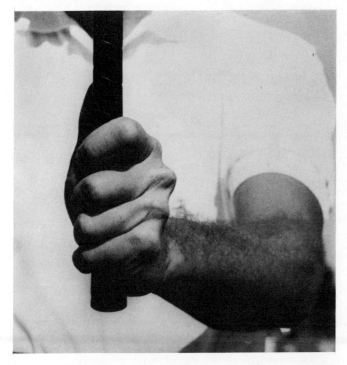

Fig. 4.   How the fingers of the left hand are aligned,
showing position of club in palm.

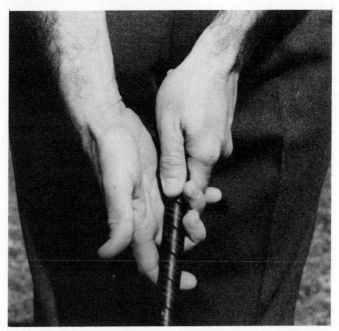

Fig. 5.   Right hand opened up to show position of club
in palm, through forefinger and across heel.

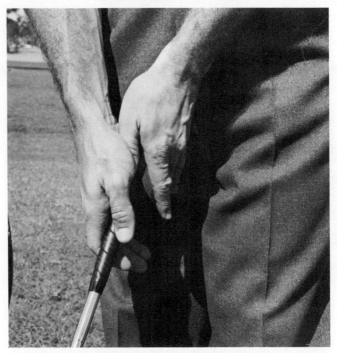

Fig. 6. Just before closing hands on the club but with palms in proper position. Note parallel position of right thumb and left forefinger.

Now take the proper grip with your left hand. (See Fig. 3.) The leather grip should run diagonally across the palm, from the heel of the palm out through the second joint of the left index finger. There should be a feeling of firmness in the last three fingers of the hand. (See Fig. 4.) The left index should be held in a crooked position, as though you are about to squeeze the trigger of a loaded gun. The thumb should extend down the shaft and lie parallel to it. The thumb position is vital in helping to unite the two hands and getting complete coordination, with the eventual position of the left thumb being somewhat determined by the right hand.

ALWAYS CHECK THE V. Check the V formed by the juncture between your thumb and forefinger of the left hand. It should point toward the joining of the neck and the right shoulder. That means that your left hand is slightly over on the shaft—not as you would hold a baseball bat. At first this will not feel completely natural because it is bound to cramp the wrist slightly, bringing into use muscles which may never have been called on before.

Believe me, as you progress in learning the game, you will find it becomes a natural action the more you play. It is the only way you can hold the club to get good results, and any deviation will eventually require

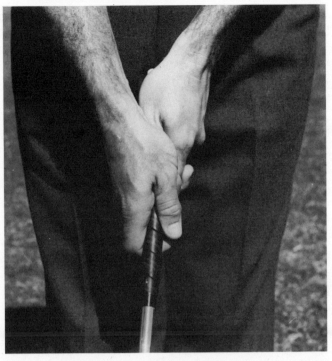

Fig. 7. A good grip—firm and compact, yet with no trace of tension.

Fig. 8. Even when club is swung up for demonstration of underside, there is no sign of stress or tightening.

laborious unlearning and relearning to get the grip back into proper position.

Some experts vow that the V should point farther over the right shoulder than the right neckline juncture, but I am inclined to disagree. The pointing of the V might vary ever so little with each individual player, but never to the left of where the right neckline joins the shoulder.

Some also advance the theory that placing the thumb straight down on top of the shaft provides greater control on the long shots. This may be true, but it requires too much know-how for the average golfer to adopt. It involves measures which properly belong to the advanced school of play— for the pros with a wide knowledge of techniques and their own shot-making ability.

THE RIGHT HAND.   Now, with the left hand in place and holding the club firmly but not tightly, place the right hand into position with fingers extended.   Bring the hand to the grip with the same motion which you might use to clap hands together at the same level.

Here, too, the club must run across the bottom part of the second finger, and with the index finger crooked, the clubshaft runs through its second joint as it is crooked.   (See Fig. 5.)   The club should come through at the midpoint of the palm.

The index and second finger, plus the thumb, are your right-hand control of the club, with the third and little fingers having very little to do except to keep the hand in position.   Be careful not to place the entire hand under the shaft, as in gripping a baseball bat.   If the right hand is in proper position the V formed by the split between the thumb and index finger will be pointing to the same spot as does the V of the left hand.

As the right hand takes position, the gripping technique which you prefer is taken by the little finger: intertwined with the left index if you are an "interlocker," or in between the left index and second finger if you use the overlap, or close to the left index if you are an "unlapper."

Again check the V's between thumb and index finger of each hand to be sure that they are approximately parallel, with neither in pure opposition as in a baseball grip.   (See Fig. 6.)   Golf requires a different holding of the clubshaft, which someone once aptly described as halfway between swinging at a baseball and chopping wood.

When the hands are in proper position, the first three knuckles of each hand should be plainly visible to the player's eyes without any movement of the head or hands whatever.   A simple check is to take the hands straight up with the club pointing in the air, the hands just out from the chest. If the correct hold has been taken, the thumbs should be in absolutely parallel alignment.

Fig. 9. The Vardon, or overlap, grip is most widely used of all.

KINDS OF GRIPS

And now to the method of joining the hands in the grip. There are three in all. The most popular and most widely used for seven decades is the overlapping grip, generally called the "Vardon." (See Fig. 9.) The late, famous Harry Vardon was not the discoverer of this method of holding the club, but he did develop it to worldwide renown at the height of his brilliant career, and thus his name became synonymous with it.

The overlap grip is taken by placing the little finger of the right hand over the index finger of the left. It is not a death lock, and the left index finger is held in slightly trigger-lock fashion.

No golf grip ever should be so tight as to strain the hands or cause the knuckles to whiten under the pressure. (See Figs. 7 and 8.) This is tremendously important in developing a good grip, though your ultimate grip must come through experimentation. It should never be so tight as to cramp the swing, nor so loose that you ever might lose control of the club, particularly at the top of the swing. It has been said that the proper grip should have the same tension you employ when you take the club from your caddy's hands. The hands should hold the club tightly enough so that it cannot be drawn from one's grasp by a slow pull, yet easily enough so that it could be jerked away with a quick yank.

Remember, too, to leave a nubbin of grip between the back of your left palm and the top of the club. An inch or so is about right. Believe me, it will guarantee better control throughout the swing and help avert the chance of losing your hold at the top.

Some players, but not many, particularly those with smaller hands, prefer the interlocking grip which follows the same general pattern as the overlap but with even firmer coupling of the fingers.

The interlock is taken by curling the little finger of the right hand and the index finger of the left. They are locked and so come off the club ever so lightly. (See Fig. 10.)

Chronologically the baseball or unlap grip might have been mentioned first, since it is the oldest and dates back beyond the written annals of golf. In this the player merely places his two hands on the shaft without any attempt to link the two units. The hands, of course, are kept as close together as possible without being uncomfortable or cramping either one. (See Fig. 11.)

Actually the term "baseball grip" is a misnomer, since here too the golfer must be sure to use the palm and finger placement of the shaft as outlined in the two other grips. In baseball, a majority of players run the club directly through both palms.

Several golfers in recent years have come up using the unlap grip and have done exceptionally well, including victories in such ranking events as the Masters tournament and PGA championship. They do not claim it is a better method, but believe that they get a little added distance by it.

The main reason they use it, despite the vast majority who favor the Vardon grip, is that they learned it as caddies and therefore it feels most comfortable to them. Believe me, they have tried experiments with the other grips, and are not too sure it would not be smart to change. However,

Fig. 10.   The interlocking grip, favored mainly by players with small hands.

that is one of the commonest feelings any golfer will have—wanting to do it some other way.   But experience teaches that a golfer should try at length to use the proved techniques.   It is preferable to force yourself to develop proper technique even at the cost of an uncomfortable feeling at the outset.

Some of the few players who use the unlap grip do so because they have unusually small hands and feel that they get a bit more power by

Fig. 11.   The "unlap," or baseball, grip.

unlocked hands. Yet the same argument is advanced by a small coterie of stars who use the interlocking grip, so the entire premise may be mental. I personally advocate the overlap grip as the surest way of acquiring genuine coordination of the two hands while offering a minimum of difficulty in learning the rudiments.

3

The Stance

So now you have the grip and should be ready to go to the second stage of learning to play golf—the stance. This, too, requires considerable preliminary instruction to make sure you get a correct start.

Actually the positioning of the feet is a bit more difficult to explain, and to keep under control, than the correct grip. There is so much leeway possible that the beginner must guard constantly against letting himself get out of kilter in standing up to the ball.

A bad stance inevitably will result in a bad swing. Unfortunately the positioning of your feet will never be automatic. It requires conscious effort to take a duplicate pattern each time you step up to the ball, and there is no absolute check point.

TAKING THE STANCE

Thus, exceeding care should be taken each time you take your stance. Try to develop a habit of placing your feet in the exact, correct position each time, and never neglect to check it visually before proceeding from there.

As you set your feet square, don't forget also to set your body the same way. The hips should be parallel to the line of the flight, and the shoulders the same way.

This may sound like useless advice but, believe me, it isn't. I have seen so many golfers set their feet in what I would consider to be an excellent position, and then crouch with their hips and shoulders as if they were squaring away for an uppercut. You must stand up to that ball, and I mean all of yourself.

A SQUARE STANCE. In the early stages of playing golf, every iron shot, from the deep-faced No. 9 to the straight-bladed No. 1, should be played from dead center between the feet. That means the ball would be on a line drawn at a right angle in the center of an imaginary line across the tip of both toes. A good working idea of this can be obtained by laying a spare club across the toes, and another bisecting it on the midline between the heels. (See Figs. 13 and 14.)

Fig. 12. Good foot position is most important.

There are five progressive movements in taking a stance; namely, club-head placement, hands on the club, adjusting the feet, setting the head, and finally, getting the body in position. The first two have been covered in the chapter on the grip, and so we go to the latter three points.

Before going into the matter of setting the feet, I would like to point out that the position you take on address will be the one which you will

Fig. 13. Use extra clubs to set up proper alignment of the feet and the clubhead.

Fig. 14. The extra clubs used to check on good address, as viewed from the rear.

have at impact, unless you let your swing go completely out of kilter. If so, you probably won't even hit the ball.

So the still, pre-swing position becomes important because it affects the moment of impact, the point of greatest stress at what is the high point of swing violence—that is, when the clubhead reaches its greatest speed. Any faults which were present at the start will be compounded many times at contact.

STANCE DETERMINES DIRECTION.   Your stance must set up the direction of the shot and this is the area of danger. I have found, through long experimentation and the old trial-and-error test, that the body as a whole has no inner sense of direction.

A player may think he is facing on dead aim at a certain target but find he is well off the bearing. The eyes help to influence this illusion. Without carefully checking, you are prone to believe you are aiming the ball at where you are looking.   But you generally will hit it where your body is aligned to propel it.   It's a case where the eyes don't have it.

I know several veterans of the tournament trail who actually take the time to plumb-bob their swings ever so often, particularly when they feel they have lost flight orientation. Invariably they discover they are well out of plumb, although they had no feeling of taking an off-line stance.

To get back to the lesson, now you have faced the club behind the ball. The spacing between you and the ball is a simple matter: just the length from your grip to the ball.

Allow yourself room for a free swing, but don't overdo it, so that you might have to reach for the ball on the downward sweep. That would entail bending the upper torso from the hips to make contact—which would be pure shot-making disaster.

Your next move is the placement of the feet, which should be done carefully and deliberately.

Here is a bit of advice which probably should be saved for the day when you have developed ability to hit the ball, but before ever taking grip, stance, or anything else, make a firm decision on the club you intend to use. You can't change clubs in mid-air, and it isn't ever advisable to try. If you have doubts about your selection, step away and rectify your error. But a well-hit shot with the wrong club will always come off better than a wavering effort because you are thinking of changing as you swing.

Of course, as a beginner you are still brandishing the No. 5 iron which was arbitrarily selected for the lesson.   Therefore, distance is not a dominant factor.   You merely want to hit the ball a solid lick.   The problem of club selection comes up later, and please bear in mind it will always be a stickler, even for the best golfers in the world.

KINDS OF STANCE.   You are taking the square stance in this lesson, which means the toes are on a parallel plane to the line of flight of the ball. Stick to squareness, although there are interesting variations which will come up for your consideration at a more advanced stage.

Fig. 15. An open stance viewed from the front. Note that the left foot is slightly drawn back.

One is the *open stance*. This is taken by moving the left foot back and the toe out slightly. (See Figs. 15 and 16.) Try it and you will see that it stiffens and reduces the action of the left side, and therefore tends to produce the slice, or left-to-right parabola of flight.

Fig. 16. The open stance viewed from the side. Note the lightly flexed knees.

Since nine out of ten golfers beyond the low-handicap class are involuntary slicers or, even worse, pushers, the new player would do well to avoid such a position. That is for the experts, and not too many of them care to fool around with it too much except when occasion demands.

Fig. 17. The closed stance, with the left foot forward, as seen from the side.

The same applies, only a little more so, to the *closed stance*. In this, the left foot is placed ahead of the line of the right foot, and the right toe is faced out just a wee bit. (See Fig. 17.)

The effect here is to strengthen the left side on the downswing, and impart a right to left flight to the ball. This is far more difficult to control and can go awry much more easily.

To explain the mechanics of the two briefly, the open or slicing stance permits the hands to get ahead of the clubface on the downswing. That will draw the clubface across the ball as it comes in contact, imparting a clockwise spin to the ball.

As soon as the stronger forward impulse eases in the distance, the spinning of the ball will make itself felt. It shows in the curl of the ball to the right at the end of flight. Veterans who know their golf use this action frequently to control the flight of the ball, which will feather down because of the air resistance. But it takes a lot of doing and a lot of control and is no shot to approach lightly or without thorough rehearsal.

The hook, in which the clubhead slightly precedes the hands on the downswing, gives the opposite spinning impulse to the ball. If it comes off perfectly, it might obtain longer distance because of the long roll which will ensue. But very few golfers, even the best, care to fool around with it.

A hooked ball can turn into a sharp ducking loop quicker than you can say Bob Jones. That's the shot the pros call a "snipe"—one which they fear wholeheartedly.

FEET AND SHOULDERS SAME WIDTH. So take that square stance and be doubly sure. The width of the feet should be just about the width of the shoulders, but it is not a hard and fast dictum. Certainly you will not be too far off if you keep the feet within this limit, or even take up an inch or two inside the shoulders.

The tendency of everyone is to spread the feet too wide. This will tend to lock the hips and cramp arm action.

As your game improves you will find the width of your stance can be modified by certain factors. These include the length of the shot you intend to hit, the depth of the club-facing you select, and the amount of energy you will expend. (See Fig. 18.) But before these come into consideration, I would say that the best placement of the feet you can take is one that feels comfortable. It is far better to have too narrow a spread than too wide.

There still are numerous details to check before you are ready to let fly at the ball. One is the position of the club in relation to the ball. The clubhead should be placed with the sole flat on the ground and with the ball in dead center.

Common sense dictates this position, since the primary address of the club at the ball represents the bottom point of the club on the downswing —the place of impact. From any other position but center, you must be able to make swing adjustments to insure a solid contact at the hitting point. Doing that brings in added muscles and nerves which should not be called on. It could put the swing completely out of kilter.

Fig. 18. The wider stance used with the long irons, with the ball addressed
slightly ahead of center, off the inside line of the left heel.

The body and its nerve-muscle system have great adaptability. You will
find you can hit the ball from almost any position, even a one-legged stance.
Trick shot players, with a little practice, can be handed the club with their
hands poised at the top of the swing and get in a good swat at the ball.

But you will not hit the ball solidly or accurately and you will not develop the automatic, fool-proof tempo so much desired by good players unless the club is correctly positioned behind the ball.

CORRECT POSTURE

Next in consideration in building a good golf game after foot placement comes body position. (See Fig. 19.) The correct posture at address is to be standing upright, but not straight up. Avoid a rigid back or any unusual stiffness. If I may be pardoned a paradox, the perfect position and set of the body should be loosely tense, but not unyielding.

A majority of the sages of linksdom agree that the best body position is one in which there is a slight feeling of sitting down. That means there should be a slight flex to the knees at address.

That doesn't mean a full bend or squat, I hasten to add. Any exaggeration of the Sitting Bull posture is a certain way of developing a flat swing—and disaster. But a reasonable loosening of the knees will help adjust the body to carry through with an easy swing action.

The position of the head should be no problem, except if any tendency to turn or move it develops. Every teacher I know feels that if the proper swing is taken, the head will take care of itself.

The head should be anchored throughout the swing, starting in a normal position to look down and see the ball as the address is taken. Don't tuck the chin in so that the ball and clubhead are out of focus. Just be natural.

On a full swing, there is a slight lateral movement of the head only in keeping with the movement of the shoulders and body going to the apex. But even so, the player should be able to halt his swing at any given point and be able to see the ball with a constant gaze.

It is a temptation to say that the head should not move at all, but this should not be a hard and fast rule. But at impact the head should be almost exactly in the same position as at address.

Keep the head down during the follow-through but not to the cramping stage. If you are conscious of any movement of the head other than its natural progression along with the body action, you must overcome it.

It isn't a matter of keeping the eye on the ball as much as keeping the head in a firm, comfortable position. Ofttimes a fellow player will say you "lifted your head," to explain a bad shot. Pay no heed to this so-called expert advice.

If your head comes up or you are "peeking" as some say, it is actually the result of a fault in your swing. Somewhere you have a hitch or a twist, or something happens which causes body distortion and resultant distortion of the head position.

It is almost impossible to circulate around locker rooms and not hear a great deal of technical palaver about the advantages of a "firm left side"

Fig. 19. Excellent posture at address of a No. 5 iron. Note the even distribution of weight, comfortable grip, easy carriage, and slightly flexed knees.

or the "left-side brace" or the "straight left arm" and on and on. Pay no attention to these mystic theories.

If they are applicable, save them until you have developed your game to a good scoring level. Once you have that feeling, you probably will try out various modifications, so let these so-called refinements go for a while. Better still, never give them any attention.

Both arms should be straight down at the address, with the upper part of the arms close in and touching the body. Don't worry about the matter of keeping the left arm straight throughout the swing. It will do that of its own volition, and any attempt to stiffen it at any point is going to ruin the entire swing.

Someone once remarked that if it were possible to interlace the arms as firmly as is possible with the fingers in the Vardon grip, then golf would be easy to master. Certainly it would assure a uniform swing throughout the up and down arcs, the ultimate and almost unattainable goal of every player.

Weight distribution should be about even on the feet, though I would not gainsay a slightly greater pressure on the left foot, since that is the fulcrum as you start the upswing and uncoil coming down.

The weight should be more on the heels to avoid toe dancing. The latter will cause loss of balance, particularly at the top of the swing, the crucial point in a good swing.

Balance is important because it insures good foot action, as necessary in golf as in the prize ring. Any competent golf professional can evaluate his pupil's game merely by watching his foot action and not even taking a glance at the swing.

THE WAGGLE

Now we have covered the essentials of the grip and address and can start the swing, but there still is a preliminary which I must mention. It will be more applicable as the lessons progress—the waggle.

Sticklers might consider this mere icing on the cake, but that is far from fact. No matter how experienced you may be or how many tournaments you may have won, the taking of a stance preparatory to hitting will build up nervous tension. That is true even with the most experienced veteran, because he too is thinking of all the factors that pertain to making a good effort and is never too sure he has covered the entire repertoire.

The one universal movement which can do much to allay this tautness is the waggle. It can manifest itself in many different ways, of course, and it is not necessary to copy any particular waggle.

It will come naturally, that preliminary action which gets you set to start the swing. Don't ever neglect to use it as a moment of contemplation, review, and preparation for the big effort.

4

The Swing

In the first stage of learning the rudiments of golf, forget all of the chatter you may hear about such things as pronation, supination, brace, wrist cock, inside hitting, weight shift, and the like. Such terms even confuse the experts and are bound to floor the uninitiated. To my way of thinking, these phrases are for locker-room discussions and good filler for magazine dissertations.

Concentrate on hitting the ball with the idea of developing your timing, and leave the fancy terms for many actions that are automatic to those who enjoy mouthing them.

POWER IS CLUBHEAD SPEED. Power is obtained from the speed of the clubhead at impact, and there is no place for an extra jerk throughout the swing. You cannot get power, which means distance, through any added body or arm twists or added violence of effort. A smooth rhythmical flowing of hands, body, and legs, all working in unison, will develop a speed and impact that will be a constant source of surprise to you in getting distance throughout your golfing life.

This principle also will be handy in your future play when your game goes awry, because you may have temporarily forgotten the absolute demand for smoothness in an effort to keep up with Jones (Tom, not Bob). When you rediscover it on the practice tee, the kinks will iron out almost automatically.

If any part of the body—hands, torso, hips, head, legs—gets out of pure synchronization at any part of the swing, the shot will come off badly.

Now that you have covered the basic elements of grip and stance, you can consider yourself ready to swing at the ball. Your No. 5 iron should be set behind the club and you have finished your waggle.

Keep in mind that the hands are the crux of the swing you are about to take. You must learn to let the body go with the hands, to be guided by them. The human body is wonderfully coordinated to work in unison with any of its components. It will perform a sequence of effort without any conscious attempt to align the order of muscular procedure.

Your swing, once started, cannot be halted in mid-air without a conscious wrench, both mental and physical. To summarize, the full action you are

Fig. 20. Starting a medium iron shot, knees bend slightly before starting club back.

undertaking is first to bring the hands up, pause to adjust for the change of direction, and then sweep the club down to the point of contact with the ball, and on to the follow-through.

The only chance you have to do any productive thinking is before you start the club. There is no time after that to change direction or technique. Therefore, once you start the club, your concentration must be on taking the swing with careful deliberation.

THE BACKSWING

The backswing is a slow, even lifting of the club to a point above right-shoulder level in the area between the tip of the shoulder and the ear. The violent portion of the swing comes on the way down, but there never should be any attempt on the part of the player to speed up the club more than the natural acceleration furnished by the body. Any such alien impetus will ruin the all-essential timing.

The first backward movement of the club should be a dragging motion as if to slide the club along, parallel to the ground. Be careful not to exaggerate this initial action at the expense of body position. Six inches, not more than eight, along the ground is sufficient drag.

Some claim the first movement on the backswing is started by the body and legs, but I believe it should be a completely unified effort by all of the components. Trying to assign any one part of the body to be the leader will throw the entire action out of time.

It should be a slow, even drag and lift. But don't make the mistake of being too deliberate or of trying to jerk the club up by easy stages. You aim to get the hands back there in a wind-up similar to the baseball pitcher's coiling to throw the ball over the plate, setting for the explosion on the way down.

The most frequently misused word in relation to golf is "relax." I think it should be applied more to the mental side than to the physical. You just cannot relax your muscles, in the true sense of the word, and still be able to build up the energy necessary to propel the ball the desired, maximum distance. Relaxation cannot mean a loose or weak hold of the club, or a flabby swing.

ARMS HANG NATURALLY. As you start back, your arms are in a natural position to hold the club, with the upper half, from elbow to shoulder, tucked in close to, but not clamped to, the body. If the arms are comfortably placed, they will take care of themselves and you will have no worry about flying elbows, falling away, and other alien movements.

Don't keep the elbows tucked in so tightly that they are cramped. If any preventive measure is necessary in this respect, it is to keep the elbows from flying out.

The elbows will adjust themselves to the various stages of the action of the swing and need no conscious manipulation other than the determination to keep them from widening out.

HEAD MOVEMENT. Let the body go with the swing without any effort to influence the movement. Your head will move, since it cannot remain set and allow the arms to go to the required height of the backswing. But it will only be a slight horizontal shift to the right as part of the whole body shift.

Fig. 21. Top of the swing with weight entirely on right leg and left leg acting as a brace. Shot is under good control, as shown by position at top of swing.

It will move equally to the left at the follow-through.

And here is some important advice that occurs in connection with the movement of your head. Pay no attention to those who comment that you lifted your head or looked up or did some other thing to explain a bad shot. It is practically impossible to do so without such severe contortion that you would feel the pain before your critic could pass out his advice.

Fig. 22. Starting down after the slight pause, weight shift has put left foot flat on the ground and hips have started to turn as hands and arms work to gain speed.

As long as you play golf, give no heed to casual, unasked advice from anyone but a qualified professional or proven veterans who know whereof they speak.

Throughout the entire swing your eyes should remain focussed on a

Fig. 23. Just before midway point on downswing. Weight has not fully transferred to right side as yet. This is about the point where top golfers start developing maximum speed to reach its utmost at impact.

single spot, probably not the ball itself but just in back of it. Make this a constant objective from the first time you swing.

BODY TURN. As your swing starts up, your right hip will turn automatically to make way for the arms to come up and the weight to shift to

Fig. 24. The ball is on its way, but the follow-through goes on. Note how weight now is entirely on left leg.

the right side. This will have a reciprocal action on the left side when you follow through.

An excellent check point on the swing will be your right knee. As you go up with the club, this knee should flex and bend slightly so that it will point just behind the ball, probably at about the same spot where your eyes will be gazing. (See Fig. 21.)

Fig. 25. Of course it was a good shot. Weight transfer is completed and hands and arms have reached a finishing position which tells an experienced observer that ball was down the middle.

The left knee also is slightly bent but not as much as the right and it will react to the lifting of weight from that side into a sort of poised position. But remember, don't come up on the left toe, as I cautioned you previously. Later on, the left knee will be pointing ahead of the spot where the ball had been as you come up on the follow-through after impact.

Many years ago the fad of getting high off the heels, practically a toe-dancing stance, became widespread. But modern swings have discarded this as too fancy and too dangerous. Nowadays the stars prefer the rolling foot action because it assures a firmer, truer, and less troublesome base of operation.

At the start of the swing, both arms are fairly straight. As you go up, the right elbow must bend and adjust to allow freeway for the hands and club. Much has been said and written of the necessity of a stiff left arm throughout this effort.

But the arm never should be rigid, as I have said before. It merely should be in position for the wrist bend which is part of the cocking of the wrists. And unless the left arm is up there at full length, the swing is bound to be foreshortened.

To visualize the general action and effect of the swing, imagine that your body is the hub of a wheel, your arms and the extended club are the spoke, and the clubhead sole is the moving rim. If you can picture this, then it is obvious that the left arm must be fairly straight to maintain the comparison with the moving rim of a wheel.

FIND THE APEX OF YOUR SWING

The top of the swing is the point you can reach without losing control of the club, or your swing control. I cannot tell you just when to stop taking the club back. Your own hands and body will find this apex with a minimum of experimentation.

The best advice I can offer here is not to go back too far or to a point where the clubhead gets far down beyond the line of the left shoulder on the other side of the body. If you can see the clubhead on your left when you are at the top of the swing, you have gone far beyond the limit of control, and the grip must have loosened at the top to allow it. Overswinging definitely means loss of control.

Every part of a golf swing from start to finish is pretty crucial, since a faulty technique or deviation at any point can ruin the flow of power which is essential. But I would say the top of the swing is the doubled-in-spades crucial moment.

The abrupt action of transferring movement from going up with the club to the important position of starting it down again toward impact will determine how well you hit the ball. In short, it will determine how well you score.

This is the point where you will cock, or bend, your wrists to get the club set to build up full speed and power at impact. The cocking is not a forward or backward bending of the wrists, but a side bend. Actually the right hand, led by the thumb, bends toward the body. The left wrist follows suit.

Fig. 26. The pause at the top, where power is gathered for the downswing.

PAUSE AT THE TOP. Every teacher firmly demands a pause at this point. Now pause is a fairly loose word. It could occupy much more of an interval than actually is required. What really is meant is that the hands, arms, and body must wait for the transfer of backward motion to get set for the downswing.

If there isn't an infinitesimal delay to accommodate this switching or re-

Fig. 27. Starting the club down. Wrinkles etched in shirt and trousers show the effort going into the action.

versal of directions, and purpose, then the player is in trouble. Probably the greatest single cause of the slice, bane of all golfers when their swing gets out of control, is starting the club down too soon.

By starting the hands before the clubhead is set, they get ahead of the

Fig. 28. Ready to turn on the heat! This is the crucial point of the swing for getting distance. From here into contact is the area where the stars generate clubhead speed.

clubhead, meaning that they progress faster. The clubhead can never catch up, and the swing will stay that way right on through impact.

It is easy to visualize the ultimate result. The clubface will be drawn across the ball instead of coming in squarely and solidly. And thus, a left-to-right spin is imparted to the ball. That produces the mechanics of a slice as the forward, outward impetus of the ball slackens, and you have a bogey or double bogey in the making unless some miracle of recovery intervenes.

SHIFTING THE WEIGHT. Much has been made by experts of the proper shifting of weight throughout the various stages of the swing. Certainly the weight will transfer to the right side as the swing goes up. Otherwise the player would topple over by the very violence of his action without any sufficient brace.

At the top of the swing the left foot has become merely a brace. All of the weight at this interval rests on a well-planted, slightly rolled-out right foot.

But don't worry about the shifting of the center of balance during the swing. That will take care of itself with automatic precision if the components are correctly aligned at the start and the body movement is smooth and measured.

THE DOWNSWING

The downswing does not require, in fact will not allow, any extra manipulation or added force. If it is started right and from a correct position, it is bound to proceed to a favorable and yard-eating contact.

It is not advisable for the beginner to try to delve into the path the club will take on the downswing, but I would like to interject here a thought which will be applicable at some time in the future.

Experts generally agree that the proper plane of the downswing should be a bit inside the plane of the club on the upswing—never outside. In fact, a majority of the bad swings you will see commit the latter error.

Once the beginner has found out how to get a modicum of distance, he must then begin to think in terms of accuracy. A famous champion once answered a critic by declaring that ability to place a spoon shot within thirty yards of the objective was pretty fair accuracy.

I think the modern stars, with the better ball and the more uniform steel-shafted clubs, can do better than this. The margin of accuracy comes down in yardage as the club faces deepen, of course.

But accuracy is not something you can will yourself to have under control. It comes from smoothness of hitting, and from practice to determine your own average of distance with the club in hand. This is an important factor in good golf. Know your clubs and know their distance potential. Since this is a variable from one person to the next, only you can make a true calibration of your own powers.

Fig. 29. Finish high and strong. If you do, the entire swing has been good
throughout.

FOLLOW-THROUGH

Never, never, never forget to follow through on your swing. Take just
as much care to finish with high hands and in a balanced position as you
used in the backswing. To the uninitiated that may sound like locking

Fig. 30. Ending of a straight-boring long iron, the body should be in good balance even after an unusually long follow-through.

the barn door after the horse is stolen, since the ball is well on its way by the time you have completed the swing.

But it will not take you long to discover that the follow-through is tremendously important because it is a telltale, a sort of visual retrospect, of your entire swing. If you have struck a good blow, your finish will be of the picture type.

If you haven't hit a good one, you can tell about it before you look down the fairway to see the ball's erratic flight. Your finishing position is the criterion.

I have done quite a bit of harping on the necessity to guard against hurrying the swing at any point. The ball isn't going to move until you hit it.

I would like to add a tricky little stunt which might give you some idea of the swing rhythm. A friend of mine has a trick of counting which he uses, particularly on tee shots, to give himself the proper top-of-the-swing tempo.

As he comes to the pause, and just going into it, at the top of the backswing, he counts to himself audibly "One-AND-two" and then lets fly. He says that is the proper chant rather than the "One-Two-Three" which many try to adapt. The fact that my friend has a broad drawl may be of some help to him.

The idea is a good one, and illustrates the point I made a while back that the pause cannot be too protracted, else the entire swing will be lost and the built-up power dissipated.

A frenzied swat at the ball will show up clearly in an off-beat finish or follow-through. Your finish, in fact, is one of the best check points in your entire swing.

But you must start thinking in terms of a good follow-through before you start your backswing. Visualize yourself finishing high and strong. You won't get a chance to think of it once you start the club back.

Make up your mind, maybe during the waggle, that you are going to try to accelerate the club all the way on up after hitting the ball. You won't be able to churn up more speed here, of course, but aiming at it will help give you speed where you need it most—at impact. Once you have reached the top of your backswing, no added propelling force beyond the normal coil-and-uncoil action of the body can be added.

You can't think that fast, or react to it if you could.

CLUB SQUARE AT ADDRESS

In recent years there has been a lot of to-do about ways of facing the club at the ball. The most vociferous have been proponents of the closed or "hooded" face at address. This coterie holds that the face, particularly of the driver, should be toed or turned in slightly before starting the backswing, and taken back in that position.

They believe the hands are inclined to open more than is necessary and that hooding will compensate for this tendency.

I do not agree. I believe the proper position at address is to put the face squarely against the ball. That is the way you want it to come into the ball, so why not set yourself correctly?

5

The Iron Clubs

You, my beginner, have gone through the routine of grip, stance, address, and swing, using a No. 5 iron at my behest. The No. 5, which splits the long-hitting irons from the pitching clubs with their deeper-face angles, can be called golfdom's average club, the in-between utility iron.

Actually I wouldn't have cared which club you might have selected as the one with which to start, since all irons should be hit exactly the same way, and from almost the same position of address.

It has been stressed by many that all iron shots are essentially pitch shots. The ball will stay in the air to a fraction of a second of the same time off each club, from the 220-yard No. 1 iron to the 60-yard wedge. Try counting from the moment of impact until the ball hits the ground and you will understand what I mean.

The difference, of course, will be the carry. The ball flies lower and longer from the straight-faced irons; goes higher and with less distance off the deep-faced ones.

Therefore every iron shot, no matter what the depth or pitch of the club face, should be hit with absolutely the same technique, procedure of address, and swing tempo.

I cannot impress this fact on the beginner too strongly. If he will digest it, and proceed accordingly, he will be off to a big head start over a lot of players who did not learn the value of developing a standard hitting pattern throughout the gamut of iron clubs.

Once the facts of iron play are appreciated, there never should be any temptation to press with the long irons, or to underhit the short ones. Those are almost universal faults among average golfers. They cannot assimilate the fact that the slant, or pitch, of the club face will get them the length they desire but feel they must add a little zing to the preconceived flight of the shot with their own muscular effort.

Conversely, the same golfers will feel too powerful on the short approaches, neglecting to take advantage of the loft and trying to steer the ball into the target, all the while loading themselves with misgivings because of their apprehension.

51

Either of these types of missed shots come from a lack of ingrained awareness that the only good golf shot is a firm one; the only good contact with the ball is a well-stroked, square-faced meeting of club face and ball.

LEARN RANGE OF CLUBS

The principal facts which must be learned in the use of the various irons are chiefly the standard distances the player will obtain with each club. Without a carefully calibrated range of personal club lengths firmly fixed in mind, the golfer cannot possibly develop consistency.

By trial and error, you should not only determine the distance you can hit with each club but also come to understand the flight action which each of the faces will impart. As you advance in hitting technique you will come to feel the difference and evaluate it almost automatically.

Just for an example, let's go down to the deepest-faced of the numbered clubs—the No. 9 iron. The wedge, of course is even deeper, but I class this club under the heading of a special weapon, which cannot be mastered until the beginner has some appreciation of solid swinging and good contact with the standard irons.

I would say my own maximum range with a No. 9 iron is about 125 yards. I probably could hit it farther, but it would involve so many extras, and so much deviation from pure form, that it would be senseless for me to try.

The 125 yards I will hit the ball is dead reckoning. I expect the ball to carry that distance and stop, with little bounce or roll.

The action of the ball when I use a No. 9 iron is quite clear in my mind, and must be that way at all times for every golfer. It will go almost straight up with very little forward impetus. On landing it will have very little or no tendency to roll because of its up-and-down flight path.

Knowing this, I can fire the shot well into the center of the target area which I fixed in my mind as I figured out the shot before taking my stance. I know I cannot go too far beyond with this club.

It must be a fully hit shot, one that I dare not spare, and I must hit it without any mental trepidation. If I think I am using too much club, or too little, then I will take another. But once I step up to a solid address, I am determined to use the club I have selected. Otherwise it would be impossible to take a full cut at the ball.

Now let's turn to the No. 7 iron. Of all the clubs in the caddy bag, I would say this is perhaps the easiest one with which to demonstrate proper hitting action to yourself by observing the air flight of the ball. Its loft gives you a good perspective, and the flight of the ball will give you a fine picture of airborne action.

The No. 7 iron, of course, belongs in the chipping category since it is much more of a control club than a distance-getting one. This may be a repetitive theme on my part, but I reiterate only to impress the point to my pupil that he or she must never try to add loft to any iron shot by any extra maneuvering of the hands or body.

Any last-second attempt to lunge down and flip the ball up in the air ruins a shot quicker than you can say double bogey, which is apt to be the inevitable result.

Partly to tick off the irons which are carried in the bag and partly to educate my reader, I am going to run through the entire kit of irons, with thumbnail comments.

IRONS IN THE NORMAL BAG. The average golfer's caddy bag should contain eight irons, numbered from No. 2 to No. 9, at least three woods, a pitching wedge, perhaps a sand wedge, and a putter. The limit of clubs which may be carried under the rules is fourteen.

Get in the habit of staying within the limit from the time you start to play. The rules say you will be penalized two strokes a hole in medal (or stroke), play for every hole on which you have played with more than the legal limit, or the loss of every hole played in a match up to and including the point of discovery. This can be pretty severe. I noticed one of the lady golf pros recently found out she had inadvertently carried an extra putter for an entire round in a major tournament and her neat 73 which would have led the field became a 91 which trailed everyone.

Fig. 31. Your kit of irons, from the wedge to the Nos. 2 and 3 (sticking out of the bag).

The tour players mostly carry about the same relative set of clubs, although sometimes one will leave out the No. 3 or No. 4 wood, depending on preference, to tote a No. 1 iron, or perhaps an extra wedge.

Sometimes they may include a special club because of the peculiarities of the particular course they are playing. In that case they will leave the No. 1 or No. 2 iron in the trunk compartment of the car in favor of a specialty club.

THE LONG IRONS

Running down the whole kit of iron clubs, I will go from the long ones down. There is no point to discussing the use of the No. 1 iron for the average player. This is a club which requires expert technique, infinite practice, and long experience to handle with any degree of safety. Leave the No. 1 iron in the clubhouse until you qualify for the National Amateur, or at least the club championship.

This theory may hold true also of the No. 2 iron, the standard long-range club of the fairway irons. The straight face and longer shaft of this club scares the ordinary golfer and may lure him into trying to give it an extra something, a sure way to hit a weak shot.

I believe the average player would do much better to depend on his No. 3 iron for the longer shots, using the same principle advocating the use of a brassie for tee shots instead of the driver. The No. 3, designed for shots from 160 to 180 yards, has loft enough to suit the eye and can guarantee some elevation without the temptation to use extra effort to get the ball airborne.

ADDRESS. I believe the position of the ball on address with the No. 3 iron still should be dead center between the feet, as it was for the No. 5 iron I advised using for those early stages of learning the game.

Once you get the hang of using long irons, I believe a little experimentation with ball position is permissible. But don't get brash. If you are going to play the ball ahead of center, don't go too far ahead. An inch is a mile here, and never forget it.

In the early stages of learning the game, I would advise teeing up the ball anywhere from a quarter-inch to a half-inch while hitting the straight-faced irons. But don't do it over so extended a period of time that it will become a habit. Almost every iron you will hit once you are indoctrinated (excepting of course those on the short holes) will be from off turf or some flat lie. So it is wise to develop proficiency of hitting from the lie which you may normally expect on your home course.

Learn to play the ball as it lies. The way you get the club into contact, avoiding either digging in too deeply or cold-topping the ball, is a crucial point in the entire operation.

Fig. 32. Addressing the No. 2 iron at dead center.

THE MEDIUM IRONS

The No. 4 iron is a club which should get you healthy yardage but also is the first one which will give you some feeling of flight control. Once called the mid-mashie, the No. 4 produces a definite loft and an easily visible zenith of flight. The ball will drop from this high point much more perpendicularly than with the straighter-faced irons, giving you a much better idea of the action in the air of a ball struck by the deeper-faced clubs.

I will pass the No. 5 iron at this juncture, since that is the club I had you start with. By now the mashie should be a fairly familiar weapon in your hands. I guarantee it will continue to be your most important club as long as you play the game.

Going to the No. 6 iron, you now are definitely in the pitching department of the game, and the most important one from the score-saving standpoint. When you consider the No. 6, you have reached the iron classification where boldness of stroking is paramount, and it is no longer necessary to make allowance for a long roll of the ball after it has hit the ground.

THE SHORT IRONS

All of the approach irons, Nos. 7, 8, and 9, and the wedge, are to be regarded as clubs which can be hit for greater accuracy. Actually, all of the irons have more target possibility than the woods.

It must be that way, since a shot at any green is aimed at a far smaller target area than are the longer shots. Almost all greens on par 4 holes are guarded either by traps, rough, or mounds, or by their own restricted entrance area. The average tolerance of an approach shot is not more than 20 yards, or 60 feet, across, which can become a bit difficult from long range. The longer par 5 holes, of course, are not as tightly guarded.

Another item in the use of irons which I would like to emphasize is the necessity to study the lie carefully. That is where your iron play gets the acid test, where good stroking asserts itself. This is particularly true when the lie is bad, such as in a hole or in someone else's divot.

The main stress here is mental. You need to learn how to overcome the urge to dig for the ball or to lift it out and up by hand or arm manipulation. No matter how good a golfer you may be, make sure you use a club you know will extricate the ball from its poor position and forget the distance.

This is important, or a bad lie can bring real trouble, not only on the particular shot at hand but in attitude throughout the remainder of the round you are playing.

You must overcome the temptation to try a heroic shot. First make sure you get results. If necessary, and this often will be the case, sacrifice that hopeful chance of getting home (i.e., to the green) by going down as many clublengths as you believe necessary to make sure of getting out of the bad lie. Think first of extricating yourself, with the hope of getting down in two strokes, meaning one putt, on the subsequent shot.

WIDTH OF STANCE. In this part for beginners, I hope you will pardon

Fig. 33. Your chipping clubs—wedge, No. 9, No. 8, No. 7.

my bringing up various theories only to tell you to put them off for later consideration. I mention them because they will crop up often in casual conversation among golfers, particularly among the average players who do not quite comprehend, as well as among the experts, who do.

One omnipresent topic is the matter of the width of the stance with the various clubs. Many of our foremost teachers advocate a narrowing of the stance as the clubs increase in pitch (or numbering).

There is no question but that the narrower the stance, the more the ball will be lofted without any extra effort. But bear in mind that you also are cutting down your ability to apply power at impact, since your arc of swing is automatically restricted by the narrower stance.

Therefore, while I might recommend future experimentation with this phase of hitting the ball, I would say to keep a normal stance of unvarying width during the preliminary stages of learning the game, as I advised many pages before when I said the feet should be placed just inside of shoulder width. This applies to the entire gamut of irons.

THE CHIPPING CLUBS. The Nos. 7, 8, and 9 irons, plus the wedges, are the standard-set chipping clubs. They are for hitting lofted shots a precise

Fig. 34.   The wedge with its wide flange on the front
of the undersole.

Fig. 35.   The No. 9 iron, without any flange and not
as deeply lofted as the wedge.

distance and are much better adapted to getting pinpoint range than the straighter-faced irons. In advanced golf they are second only to the putt in the stroke-saving department.

All three of these approach clubs are primarily intended for the chip-and-run shot, without too much run. But they also can be manipulated to give wide diversity in their use. These refinements of use, however, should be put off until the beginner has achieved proficiency in their normal use.

The chipping clubs also are the great reliance for recovering from deep rough. Here one uses a swing halfway between an axe and a hatchet stroke. They also are the medium for getting out of sand in traps or rough and sundry other trouble shots, which unfortunately occur all too frequently.

The range of these clubs is from 60 to 140 yards, or maybe 150. But when you are just starting to play, I believe the clubs should be played far shorter than these distances, with the idea in mind of working up to the added length after control has been attained.

Below these standard, numbered clubs comes the wedge, even deeper-faced and unquestionably more accurate. There are quite a number and variety of wedges to select from, since each of the better-known manufacturers tries to personalize his make. But I would advise picking up one with a real broad flange on the sole—as broad as you can find.

This is the club's advantage, because the facing of the sole will enable the club to slide through underneath the ball rather than digging in as happens on a similar shot with the narrower-edged No. 9. That built-in bounce is the key of good wedge play.

Approach your initial efforts with the wedge with extreme caution. It is a great stroke-saver, but also a difficult weapon to master. In fact, I don't believe it ever is gotten completely under control by any golfer, no matter how experienced he may be.

It will do no harm, and might result in added effectiveness, to choke down a bit on the grip when using the chipping clubs, since distance is not the vital objective. I would say the heel of the left hand, which is uppermost in the grip, should be about an inch and a half below the end of the shaft.

This choked grip not only will give the player better control, but will add confidence. It narrows the arc of swing, of course.

CHIP SWING IS DIFFERENT. I said before that the swing with the chipping clubs is the same as with the longer irons, but there is a slight difference, even so. Since these clubs have shorter shafting, you will find yourself standing a bit more over the ball, with the eyes looking down more perpendicularly when in the position of address.

That naturally means you must take more of an upright stroke, both backward and forward, but I do not believe this should be done by pure intent. From the position of stance and address over the wedge, your arms and body will take care of this slightly changed trajectory of swing without any conscious volition on your part.

An important thing to remember is that you must never beat down on any chip shot. The positioning of the ball, and I recommend a center address throughout, should be the key of your swing action.

THE TRICKY WEDGE

Unless you are reading this lesson in England, or the golf courses in your area are unwatered and hard, let the chip-and-run shot bide awhile. The one club you cannot avoid taking up all too soon as you get into this game is probably more difficult to control than any other club—and I mean the wedge.

The use of this club, particularly the pitching wedge, is so important that I want every pupil to start working on it as soon as possible. Believe me, it takes some doing to master this club. In fact, you may never be absolutely certain of it, nor will any other golfer. The best that even the Palmers, Caspers, and Littlers can hope for is greater proficiency and a reasonable total of good results.

To reiterate, I would advise the purchase of a wedge with a real broad flange on the sole, as broad as you can find in the club rack. This is the advantage of the club—that sole. That is what causes the clubhead to slide through, in under the ball and prevents digging down. You will find out how important this can be as your swing develops.

The bounce caused by the flange is your advantage with this club, and also your problem, one which you must adapt by extended trial and error. You should tend to pick up the wedge a bit more than you would a standard club, and perhaps a wee bit faster.

The wedge, of course, has great loft, and any hand action you might try to add in order to scoop the least bit will result in a real blooper. The wedge shot must, of all things, be firm. Never try to use special grip or posture on this one, especially in the novice stage.

You probably will produce some of the bloopiest, most unsatisfactory shots in the realm of golf at the outset. But don't worry. Even the finest players in the world do the same thing, not once in a while but frequently.

VARIATION OF ADDRESS. In playing the wedge, you should take a narrower stance than with the longer clubs. If so minded, you can play the ball back of the dead center position between the feet, but not much.

Earlier I tried to set a hard-and-fast rule about centering the ball, and

Fig. 36.   Address for a wedge shot. Ball is slightly back of center, feet close
together.

I believe the beginner would do best to follow these instructions to the
letter. But as your game develops, it will be possible to try adjustments.
The wedge is the first club where such variation is not only permissible
but necessary.

The hands and arms should be held fairly close to the body on the

Fig. 37. The wedge is brought up quickly without appreciable shifting of body.

address with a wedge, not touching but comfortable. There should be some bend at the waist but no resemblance to a crouch. If the left arm and club shaft feel firmly continuous, with the right hand serving more as a guide and just little bent at the elbow, then you have good wedge-shot position of address.

Fig. 38. Top of wedge swing never should be beyond shoulder height. Notice that hips have not turned.

The shot is a hand effort, with the wrists pivoting freely. The arms should not intrude too much, and the backswing must be slow. The top of the swing is the crucial point as in any other swing, setting up as it does for a downswing that is firm rather than fast or power-laden. Guard against any tendency to overswing.

Fig. 39.   Weight still is equably distributed on downswing and body position
has remained almost constant throughout.

The body remains in a fairly constant position, with very little shifting
of weight or any attempt at the pivot which is so vital in long shots.

The hands apply power at impact, but there should be no effort to churn
up clubhead speed as in distance hitting. Distance here is controlled by
the amount of backswing. A 30-yard pitch over a trap involves the same

amount of conscious effort as a 60- or 70-yard shot. The difference is the extent the club is taken back—longer for the long shot, of course.

This is the trial-and-error part of your practice with this club, among other things. As I have said before, and wish to repeat with emphasis, the wedge is not an easy club to master. But all the effort you may choose to expend in learning to use it will be doubly repaid, and more, in future stroke-saving.

PROS CONCENTRATE ON WEDGE. The next time you go to a tournament where the big stars are playing, take a stroll out to the practice area. There you will see that most of them devote as much time practicing with the wedge as they do with all the other clubs in the bag.

There might be an exception here and there, a fellow who may have had a particularly poor previous round with a No. 3 or a No. 7 iron or the like. He will be boning up on that club, of course, but he never will neglect a session with that chipping wedge either.

All of the top-notch players carry two wedges. One is for pitching off fairways, out of the rough, and on all grassed areas close up to the green. The other wedge will be for special use in sand. Basically the two clubs are alike. If you acquire skill with one, you will have little or no trouble with the other. The main difference will be that the sand wedge will have a sharper front edge, less loft and more weight.

The follow-through is just as important in the chip shot as with the longer irons. But it should not go any farther through than the hands went back on the backswing. Here again, I say of the follow-through that it is not something to aim at, but the perfect check point of your swing. If you have hit the ball well, then your follow-through will be exemplary.

CHIPS MOSTLY FALL SHORT

I really don't know which is the more discouraging result when you miss a chip shot—the little fluffed ball which just pops ahead of the club weakly, or the fiercely sculled shot which scoots out of control because the edge of the club made the hitting contact with the ball.

Both of these types of misses stem mainly from lack of confidence in one's swing. A last-moment decision by the player that too firm a blow might send the ball beyond the objective, a common plague with all golfers, ruins swing timing completely.

Only rarely will a chip shot go disastrously beyond the target. The more likely chance is that it will fall short. Yet even the top-ranking stars, who know this, will sometimes flinch. "Never up, never in" is a favorite expression applied to putts which are short, but is more applicable to the average chip shot.

As you progress in learning the game, you can ultimately consider the so-called "squeeze" shot with the wedge. But don't delve into this difficult facet of wedge play until you have mastered the basic swing.

Let me repeat again and again that the wedge requires practice, practice, practice. Only by demonstrating to yourself what you can do with this club will you ever get control of it, and I might say vice versa to that, too.

Believe me, you will hit a lot more bad ones than you will good ones with the wedge at the outset. But remember what I remarked a while back about the good players at practice. They never stop working on their approach game.

6

The Woods

I have purposely left consideration and discussion of the wood clubs until this chapter, mainly because the woods are more difficult to master. I would not advise any beginner to try his hand at any of the wood clubs before he has learned at least the rudiments of swinging the irons.

The swing used with any of the wood clubs is precisely the same as with the irons, so therefore I will not attempt to review the building-up processes of the swing at this point. Yet there is a subtle difference in playing the woods which can be felt, yet is almost impossible to explain, or even to demonstrate.

First off, your woods are designed, or at least fashioned, for distance. They have longer shafting, for one thing, which is bound to give them a slightly different feel in the hands. This, of course, has a direct affect on the swing.

I say that you should use the same technique with the woods as you do with the irons, but you will take a wider arc of swing with the woods because of their construction. It is not a pronounced variation, however, so don't ever look to change your swing by conscious effort.

The major variation between woods and irons, perhaps, is the bottom of the wood clubs. This underside, or sole, is flat and usually the size of the wooden head itself. Thus the underface of the club has much more area coming in contact with the surface from which you are hitting than even the wide-flanged wedges have.

The woods, of course, are designed for playing off the fairway when you need a long carry, with room also for a longish roll. The woods require much more precision and control since a long bad shot is bound to go much more wrong than a short-iron shot struck the same way and with the same force.

There are exceptions, of course, but only in the field of advanced wood technique. As with the irons, I will discuss the major variations in stroking, but I strongly recommend that the beginner hold off in trying these refinements until some skill has been developed with the woods.

Fig. 40.   Dow Finsterwald ready to tee off, his favorite
driver set for action.

THE FOUR STANDARD WOODS

A standard set of woods, such as you might buy off the rack in the pro
shop, is composed of four woods, numbered 1, 2, 3, and 4. The number
designates the slope of the hitting face of the club. Before the modern
steel-shafted clubs were developed, these clubs corresponded respectively to
the driver, brassie, spoon, and wooden cleek, the latter being distinguished
from the old pitching cleek, an iron.

The last-named clubs—No. 4 or wooden cleek—may not be counterparts.
Veterans who go back to the days of hickory shafts tell me the No. 5 wood,

a specially made club recently rising in popularity with club players, comes nearer to resembling the old-time wooden cleek.

The top players do not regard the No. 5 wood as anything but a toy and you seldom will find one in the caddy bag of a touring pro. He can do so much better with an iron at the same range that he would not waste the space in his caddy bag. Yet the average player, especially one who lacks consistency with long irons, might try out the No. 5 wood as an experiment.

The driver is the longest-hitting of all clubs, with a face which is almost straight—it slopes at an angle of only 11 degrees from the absolute perpendicular of 90 degrees. To the naked eye, this may appear to be little or no loft, but it is nonetheless sufficient to raise a well-hit ball to sufficient height. The driver is a difficult club to master, and even the finest players sometimes lose their touch with it.

The driver is designed for hitting the ball off a tee; never forget that. Any time you are using a driver, be sure you set the ball well up off the ground.

I have heard it claimed that a good player with confidence in himself can let the driver "sweep" a bit when going for distance. That means, of course, that the swing can be a bit flatter, thus automatically insuring a wider swing arc.

I would not say that this idea has no merit, but I caution anyone but an experienced player to be extremely wary of attempting any variations, even minor ones. I find the driver difficult enough to keep on target with a normal swing without attempting any tricks with it.

I do not think a beginner should even pick up a driver and start flailing away. Hold off on this club until you are satisfied you have acquired some facility with the deeper-faced woods.

THE MORE LOFT, THE SAFER THE CLUB. The No. 2 wood, or brassie, with its greater loft, or a No. 3 wood, with even more slope in the face, will prove much more efficient, much more accurate, much less troublesome, and much safer for the novice. I might add that this holds true right up through to the top-drawer players. With the clubs of greater loft the cost in distance, which is much less than most people think, will be more than recompensed by the greater accuracy attained. It is more important to put a wood shot in the fairway at 200 yards than to hit it 250 yards and into a half-unplayable lie in the rough.

The No. 2 wood has a loft of 14 degrees, three more than the driver. It isn't much, but even this is an aid to accuracy by helping the ball to rise as it leaves the hitting face.

Never, and I mean *never*, try to help a wood club get the ball up. The natural pitch of the face must do that as you strike the ball as nearly perfectly as you can. If you cannot get results that way, then go to a deeper-faced wood—or take an iron.

The No. 3 wood, or spoon, has a relatively deeper pitch to the face (16 degrees), a pitch which the novice can detect with the naked eye. This is the old, tried and true club, the one which does the job, particularly for beginners. The ball cannot fail to fly up as it is hit, even though the player's technique may not be well developed. If you cannot get some height with this club, then you need helpful advice and some changing of your swing pattern.

I would say the No. 3 wood is the club that is best to use as you introduce yourself to the art of playing the woods, which is moving into the refinements of good golf. Get so that you can hit a reasonably good shot with a No. 3 wood, and then you can safely turn to the straighter-faced woods without fear.

Inserting a strong bit of advice at this point, I would like to impress on all golfers that you never should try to hit a brassie from the fairway unless it lies extremely well. Never try to hit a No. 2 wood from the rough or a poor fairway lie. If the ball does not lie well, meaning that it is sitting up off the ground on firm turf, reach for your No. 3 wood by all means.

The No. 4 wood with its 19 degrees of loft has deeper facing than the No. 3. Here an argument might be churned up that the No. 4 is a better club for the beginner than the No. 3. Certainly it is much safer to hit from a poor lie.

For the beginner, I might be inclined to admit that the No. 4 wood is a saner club for primary practice. It is lighter and has a smaller head, and therefore it will be easier to swing and follow through and the ball will rise faster.

But it is not a long-distance club, being more fitted to hit the high, floating type of shot. It is this action which sometimes makes it a preferred choice over its counterpart among the irons, the No. 3 iron. In any case of doubt, use the No. 3 iron in preference for better impact and greater control.

As to hitting a wood shot from anything but a good lie, I am sure any pupil will appreciate the point once he gets to hitting the woods. Not even the finest players are careless in their club selection or technique when the ball lies badly. The sole aim at this juncture is a good recovery, not a miracle.

There is also the No. 5 wood, which I mentioned before and which recently has grown in popularity, particularly among older golfers. It has the same loft of 21 degrees that a No. 2 iron has, but will not propel the ball as far. Oddly enough, the No. 5 wood appears to have undoubted "raising power," even to the least initiated golfer. Yet he will view the No. 2 iron, having the same slope of face, with great distrust, fearful of his ability to get the ball in the air. He will tend therefore to try to give the No. 2 iron added lofting impetus and probably ruin the shot. The No. 5 wood is not a standard club in regular sets, but mainly a sort of "trick" club which is not at all essential to a good player or even the average hitter. He can do more with irons in the same distance range and keep better control of the ball.

The No. 5 wood is something of a mental crutch for players who lack confidence. It is a bad club to depend upon. I know golfers who have had special No. 6 and No. 7 woods made up for themselves—maybe just to be different. Do not attempt to follow this fad.

No golfer can control a wood club shot as well as he can an iron of the same distance. Therefore the No. 5 wood should be considered excess baggage which might displace a more useful club in the caddy bag if you want to keep within the fourteen-club limit set by the Rules of Golf.

In summary, the standard loft for the woods—meaning the angle of slant of the hitting face of the club—is given in the following tabulation. In standard woods for ladies the degree of loft is one higher for each club.

No. 1 (Driver)	11 degrees
No. 2 (Brassie)	14 "
No. 3 (Spoon)	16 "
No. 4 (Spoon)	19 "
No. 5 (Spoon)	21 "

DISTANCE IS AUTOMATIC. Never consciously try to get distance with any of the woods, and this holds for veterans as well as beginners. The distance will come automatically if you swing well at the ball and your timing is good. Any attempt to add impetus to your swing is apt to throw the entire action out of kilter.

I might add that in my opinion a player who might, by some manner or means, develop ability to hit the same wood club varying distances probably would be hurting his game because he would always have that nagging doubt in his mind as to what was the right distance to hit the ball.

It is difficult enough to hit a solid wood shot every time up, and any attempt to manipulate the swing to control distance is bound to kink the action.

TIPS ON HITTING THE WOODS

The backswing is the crux of a good wood shot. The basis of a good backswing is to get the left hand, left arm, and left knee all working together as you start back. If you can attain a uniform flow of motion with these three components, you have a good swing going.

TOP OF THE SWING. The critical point of the swing, and this holds particularly true in the woods, is the top of the swing. Here the pause that

Fig. 41. On the tee for the big hit! Stance is square, grip easy, and body in position for coiling on a long swing.

rallies all the muscular and neural facilities for the strong swing down is vital.

Any attempt to hurry the shot down means complete ruination of your effort. It is the reason that all experts advocate the slow, smooth starting-back of the club, and why they pursue the same regimen themselves.

Never try to force the clubhead under the ball to get added loft with the wood shots. These clubs need more precise contact of face and ball than the irons. Generally speaking, the impact should be at the exact bottom of the swing, meaning that the front sole edge of the club should be flicking the turf at the split second it is coming in contact with the ball.

This precision may not be quite so necessary with the irons, and there is some variation possible with the different woods, too. With the No. 4 wood, for instance, the feeling should be of hitting the ball a faint bit on the side of the downward swing. The loft of the club face will take care

Fig. 42. Starting the club back with rapid shifting of weight to right leg and side. Left arm is straight, and head holds firm position.

of getting the ball up. This applies, of course, to a shot from a cuppy or deep lie particularly.

As I have said before, golf improves as it becomes more of a habit, which is the case with most other things we learn by practice. It is just as easy to develop a good habit as a bad one.

STARTING A HOLE. "You cannot play a hole any better than you start it," goes an old golfing adage. It may hold true, but I would say there should be some added interpretation of these words. I don't believe it means every drive must be over 300 yards. What it conveys is that the drive must put the player in position to make a good second shot. I maintain that position is a more important factor in driving than distance.

If you hit a good tee shot as to position—that is, placement which will open up the hole for an earlier approach—and with good technique, you

Fig. 43. Top of the swing shows tight coiling of body, ready for downward swing and shift of weight to left side after impact. Note flexed left knee pointing slightly beyond ball.

have set yourself up to play all the necessary shots well. You have established a feeling within yourself of confidence and ability to hit the next shot well.

That is an important factor in playing golf, which is more mental than physical in many ways. It certainly helps to induce the relaxation which is so essential to obtain good timing.

PRACTICE FOR A REASON

I would advise the beginner to spend a lot of time at practice with the woods, a bit of advice which may apply only to them. Experienced golfers need no persuasion to get out there and hit practice woods. The ball gets so much distance and flies so beautifully that veterans enjoy sessions with

Fig. 44. At impact, weight has started to go on left leg, but body is "behind" the ball for maximum delivery of power.

their wood clubs just to watch the ball fly out so far. It can be overdone too, at the expense of work on other clubs.

My advice would be to refrain from practicing wood shots for the sheer esthetic pleasure of watching the ball fly into the wild blue yonder. Rather, any sessions with the wood clubs should be for definite reasons, such as correcting a fault which may have shown in playing your most recent round, or developing better techniques, or taking a fast warm-up before starting a round. In the latter case, only a few solid cuts at the ball are necessary to give one's self the proper playing tone.

To illustrate the point suppose I told you to take a pop at the ball with your driver. It whips out with a wide slice. I could then say to you, "That's your lesson for today," without being curt or facetious. The flight action of that drive should have taught you something.

That shot happens to be a roundhouse slice into the rough off the right

Fig. 45. With the ball on its way, Dow's uncoiling and follow-through illustrates effort put into the shot even more than was shown in the downswing.

side of the fairway. It should have told you that your timing was off and that more than likely your hands were away ahead of the clubhead at impact. Pursuing the theme, it means you were starting down too soon by committing the common error of not waiting at the top of the swing. It means you have some work ahead of you to correct the error before strolling to the first tee.

A player in the slicer's predicament perhaps needs some good advice from a competent teacher at this point. However, if the player himself has a good grounding of practice and instruction, he can evolve the steps necessary to overcome the transient flaw.

As you progress in the game, test yourself mentally to see how much you have really learned by trying to dissect your own swing, to analyze any flaws which might be hurting your swing. It could be a considerable help to you in the future because your ability to improve depends on yourself alone. The more you know of corrective methods, the better you will play.

FLAWS, AND THEIR CAUSE

I said that the usual cause of a slice comes from not waiting at the top of the swing. I could be wrong, since there are a number of other things which can produce the roundhouse shot. However, the hurrying-up of the downswing will usually be present when a slice is hit. The variance may be in other actions during the swing which cause it to go wrong.

The swing continually requires coordination of the body, a basic law which cannot ever be bypassed. Relaxation is essential.

The woods should be hit from a dead-center position between the two feet (see Fig. 46). Some players are convinced they get better results by getting a little behind the ball on the drive, where you have the advantage of a teed-up ball and aim to help in getting the ball in the air as it leaves the tee. I would say the position of the ball is a matter of personal choice, but only after trial-and-error practice to determine the best position of address. It never should be exaggerated the slightest bit.

Don't ever attempt to correct one fault by committing another. The

Fig. 46. Addressing a fairway lie with a No. 3 wood. Notice loft of club in relation to ball.

Fig. 47. Left hand, arm, and knee should be in unison on backswing. Here Dow is going back for a fairway wood shot using a slightly closed stance which requires faster turning of the right hip.

chain reaction of mistakes is too dangerous. Try to work on one fault at a time. Deviations from the normal swing are bound to creep into one's game. My par-busting associates on the tour, without a single exception, have been in the throes of such an experience and have undergone the sometimes painful, usually slow process of finding the fault and correcting it.

No player can attain more than momentary perfection in hitting a ball.

Fig. 48. Critical point! The top of the swing is
where you pause but never tarry.

Fig. 49. Neither hands nor arms should show
any signs of tension at the top of the swing.

It is a good trick if you can hit two near-perfect shots in a row. One of the most proficient golfers of them all, who practices far more than any player, seldom is satisfied with shots which observers might consider flawless.

There is an interesting point about working on swing flaws. Veterans have found that while working on one phase of correction, they frequently cure another secondary fault automatically without ever trying to fix it up.

Be constantly determined that you will keep your head "behind the ball," so to speak, which means not allowing your head to lead the clubhead into the hitting area. But don't overdo it. Getting your hands ahead too far creates the drag motion which produces the slice, probably golf's most universal error. Your hands must lead on the downswing, but only up to the point where you start the wrist snap that gives power to the shot at contact.

The hook, of course, comes from the reverse action, letting the clubhead get ahead of the hands. But few beginners will be troubled by this.

Don't get to worrying about cocking the wrists, or any other of the mystic things which golfers sometimes spout about trying to explain the mechanics of the swing. If you have a smooth, even flow, the wrists cock naturally, and timing will take care of itself.

With the hope that it will not confuse the beginner, I must add that only a few of the top-ranking players carry a brassie in their bag, mainly because they must remain within the legal limit of 14 in the caddy bag.

The circuit golfers feel that if they need distance on the fairway, they can get it just as easily with the driver from the same lie. They would never be tempted to use either the driver or brassie from a poor lie, for one thing.

Once the technique of hitting a driver is learned, the straighter-faced club can be used just as effectively. Actually the difference between the loft of the two clubs is not too great. However, in the case of the better golfers, techniques can be used to get the ball in the air with the driver. But don't ever try if you don't know how.

Just as the average golfer would do much better to use a brassie off the tee, and leave his driver in the locker, so would he get better results using a No. 3 or No. 4 wood off the fairway. He might not get the distance he wants, but he will get quicker loft and a truer flight with the deeper-faced clubs.

On the tour, you often will hear a player explain a good round by saying, "I kept the ball in play." That is an expression meaning that trouble was avoided frequently by hitting a lesser club than the distance demanded because of a poor lie, or too much of a gamble with trouble. Experienced hands know full well that better scores can come from good placement than from sheer distance.

In fact, the beginner and a majority of high-handicap golfers probably would get much more satisfactory results if they used a No. 3 wood off the tee, a facet which I will discuss at greater length subsequently.

7

Putting

Putting is the fine art of golf, the department where you can save the most strokes and where you may win or lose a tournament. According to the American par, as distinguished from the English bogey, a course rated at par 72 is played fifty per cent on the putting surface since 36 strokes, or two putts per 18 holes, are automatically allowed on the greens.

The playing professional who takes the full quota of putts knows he cannot hope to remain in contention. The green is the one part of the course where he has more than a reasonable chance to save shots.

There are some who hold that a good putting touch is an inherent gift, an innate talent which you have or don't have. I do not subscribe wholly to such a theory although I am convinced some players have a feel for the delicate art above and beyond normal touch.

But I also believe that it is possible for any player to acquire a good stroke on the greens, which means good results. It is not achieved by mere wishing or by a few casual sessions on the practice green, but by patient effort to acquire correct habits.

My putting lessons, therefore, are directed to the golfer who may not possess that extra bit of smoothness, judgment, and serenity which gets the ball into the cup faster and oftener than most. It is a wonderful gift, for sure, but even the putting magicians must observe the basics.

This I have observed in years of competition—almost every great putter I ever have seen tends to use an entirely orthodox grip, a technique of stroking which obviously is well rehearsed. He also is a man of considerable patience.

DON'T TRY ANY TRICKS. Right here, I would like to make a strong point. I am solidly certain that no one ever can putt consistently well using a trick method of holding the club or placing the feet. There are exceptions, as to every rule, but in the long run, good form will be a dominant factor in good putting. It is worse being an in-and-out putter, who cannot miss one day and cannot hole a two-footer the next, than to be an average performer on the greens. Nothing can be as upsetting as an inconsistent putting blade. Illustrations of this are legion.

The secret of good, consistent putting is a good sound grip, stance, and stroke. If you concentrate on developing all three, your putting is bound to improve, although there is no guarantee that you will move into the exalted realm of the greens immortals who have that extra something.

There have been great golfers who never did become as proficient on the green as they were through the fairway. Experts say some of these unfortunates might never have lost had they been able to putt as well as they could hit woods and irons. Yet I do not believe this. If they had not adhered to the principles of good gripping, solid stance, and even stroking, they might never have won at all. They had to hole a few when they did win, so they were not completely baffled at all times.

FRETTING WILL RUIN ANY PUTT.   There is an important factor of good putting which I have not mentioned—the mental side. I delayed mentioning it because I believe good nerves can be developed after an orthodox style of execution has been achieved.

The worst possible thing you can do is fret over any putt, fearing you will not be able to sink it. Doubts and worries occupy the mind instead of the single-minded purpose of getting that ball in the hole—call it concentration or what you will.

The mental side of putting is a difficult realm for a teacher to invade. There is no way of defining the exact amount of mental stress involved nor is there any chance for the teacher to prescribe the exact amount of relaxation which is necessary.

To be a good putter you must learn how to eliminate extraneous thoughts and concentrate on the job at hand. That is to hole the putt or, if it is a long one, to get the first putt near enough to guarantee an easy hole-out.

An inches-away second putt can do amazing things to your ease of mind because it will take you to the next tee relaxed and serene. Conversely, a poor approach putt and a missed second one can build up a lot of tension which might ruin subsequent tee and fairway shots.

The important point to remember in learning to putt is to train yourself to develop a pattern of stroking which will be exactly the same on every putt. No one can vary from one putt to the next and remain consistent.

There is no single blueprint I could lay down for all putters to use. Within the bounds of orthodoxy there can be many variations of grip, stance, and stroke. The technique which you adopt, and work to achieve, should be simple and smooth. Develop a uniform style, and stick to it.

I admit there are times when you will want to experiment by trying a variation of the method you have set for yourself. Every golfer, no matter how adept, comes to such a time when his blade seems to be beyond control and nothing goes right.

But even in such extremity, the adjustment of one's stroke should be only just enough to find out if a little difference in manipulation might overcome the slump. Be on continual guard against any radical changes on an experimental basis. If you want to change, do it completely and without any thought of ever returning to the old style.

THE RIGHT PUTTER TO USE

There are infinite varieties of putters of all shapes, weights, sizes, and colors. I would not attempt to recommend any one type of head to any player, except to warn against the extremes. The odd heads and such weapons as the one designed to hit from between the legs, croquet style, are for faddists.

The basic putting weapon, of course, is the regulation blade putter, with a head forged very much like the other standard irons but with a straighter face and more upright shafting.

I guess the most popular putter now in use on the circuit is an adaptation of the straight blade, but with center-shafting. It generally is known as the bull's-eye, with a bronze head and a little curlicue on the blade in back of where the shaft is attached to the head. Outside of the fact that it is beautifully made, the advantage of this club is that it gets the player more over the ball in a more upright stance.

The opposite of the blade is the so-called mallet head, a club with a broader beam. This club, too, has center-shafted variations but the latter are by no means as popular. More than 50 years ago, however, the first American ever to win a British title used a center-shafted mallet, called the Schenectady, to capture the British Amateur. The indignant British thereupon barred any center-shafted club for several decades, although they still were legal in this country. Now there is no ban on the shaft coming out of any portion of any putter.

There are blade putters with flanges in the back to give a broader surface on the bottom and infinite variations from there. Steel, bronze, brass, aluminum, and even wood are used in the heads. Some jewelry firms even have sterling silver and 14-carat gold putting heads.

In the face of so much equipment, about all that I can recommend to a pupil is to heft all sorts of clubs until one is found which feels good in the hands. Every pro golf shop has a rack of putters of all varieties.

Right here let me warn my pupils to beware of too much weight in the head. As your game develops, you will acquire more and more feel for your favorite putter. Too heavy a head will retard this development.

THE GRIP

The method of gripping can be, or should be, a personal choice. It should be comfortable, and standard enough to be firm. The placing of the hands is the important factor, making sure that the club shaft is well under control at all points of the putting swing.

I myself prefer the reverse overlap grip, which means putting the forefinger of the left hand over the little finger of the right hand (see Fig. 50). Otherwise the placing of the hands on the shaft is similar to the grip you take with any fairway iron. This is possible because you need no power in a putting stroke, and taking away a strong grip with the left forefinger therefore is permissible.

My reasons for using the reverse overlap are threefold. First, I want to make sure of a firm hold on the club without being overtensed. Second, I want to make sure of complete unity of action of the hands. Third, I give my right hand a little more control of the swing action by having the little finger on the leather.

In general I would recommend the reverse overlap to most golfers, sight unseen, and steer away from the interlock or overlap. But I certainly would not want to make a hard-and-fast rule about it. I have seen too many wonderful putters who employ grips which are, let us say, personalized to propound any one method as the only way.

The only warning I might issue at this point would be to guard against developing some tricky kind of procedure. I have in mind such a style as the pendulum stroke which some extremists have tried temporarily. The left hand grips the club at the foot of the leather, while the right hand takes hold at the tip of the club. Thus the left hand acts as a fulcrum with the right hand providing the momentum. The croquet stroke is another.

As a player who sometimes loses his own touch, I can understand why a player might experiment with such a departure. The greens touch can come so fast and vanish so rapidly that a fellow who has enjoyed a spell of holing them out can go almost insane waiting for the velvet to return to his finger tips. Over a prolonged period of blues on the green, a player gets to the point of being willing to try anything to get back the old touch, or to develop a new one.

Also, when a good player's blade goes bad, he develops considerable added tension and is looking for any possible means to relieve the pressure.

I recall that a famed veteran once won an Open on Long Island while putting with one hand; his right, I believe. He must have been another who was overplagued. But you can bet he did not stick to the one-armed method long. It was a rare instance of an extreme technique clicking, and he certainly would not recommend it to anyone else.

There should be no tenseness in a putting grip, yet the club must be held firmly. It is important that the face of the putter be kept uniformly straight across the line of the putt to the cup, or to the apex of the turning point of "borrow" in the case of a sidehill putt.

Fig. 50. The reverse overlap grip, with the forefinger of the left hand on top of the little finger of the right (thus reversing their position in the normal overlap grip).

This is a point I would like to emphasize. One of the finest and most consistent putters on the tournament circuit has a simple, uncomplicated style and technique which has been closely studied by his fellow pros. There is general agreement within the fraternity that his stroke guarantees less chance of going awry than that of almost any other rival. He may not sink as many spectacular putts as some of the velvet strokers, but his average

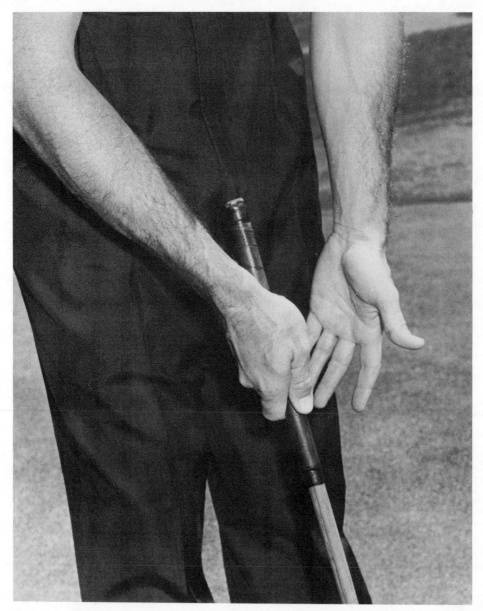

Fig. 51. The left hand should be placed on the putter easily and without tension
after first putting the right in a comfortable position.

over a series of tournaments will equal or surpass many of the inspired
strokers.

I think the essence of this player's considerable putting talent is his
unusual ability to keep the face of his putting blade square to the line down
which he intends to stroke the ball. That may not necessarily be the line
between the ball and the cup, since he might be putting for a "borrow."

Fig. 52. The putting grip must be fairly loose but firm enough to keep the face of the club steady on the mark. The thumb down the shaft helps to insure firmness.

This to me is the basic movement of good putting, and is the reason that I offer a personal choice of methods of gripping. I say take the one which will keep that club face firmly on the line of the putt and allow no deviation or rotating action.

THE GOOD PUTTING SWING

Like every golfer who makes his living at the game, I have given a great deal of thought to the art of putting and to developing a sure-fire technique. I have been reasonably successful and therefore I will try to pass some of my hard-earned experience along to you.

The putting procedure which you might undertake naturally at the beginning of your golf might not be the best one for you by any means. Some experimentation would be indicated here, plus considerable observation of many styles. All I can say is to bear in mind constantly that the putting stroke always is open to adaptation and improvement.

Just for instance, let's consider the various stances. Many players find they are more consistent with the so-called brace stance. That means planting the left leg straight and firm with all the weight on it and putting against this solid wall. The right foot rests lightly, and sort of drags in comparison to the strong left side.

Others prefer the center, evenly balanced stance, where the weight is distributed equally on both feet planted to eliminate any tendency to pivot. In this, the player is able to get over the ball more than any other way.

One of the superior bladesmen of the pro tour favors the center stance and advocates what could be called shoulder putting. It consists of swinging with the shoulders moving laterally, while the arms and hands serve as a semirigid extension of the shaft of the putter to the shoulders.

The putting stroke should have pure uniformity throughout—no jerks and no jabs. The length the club is taken back is dictated by the distance between your ball and the hole, an art which must be acquired by practice and experience.

Experts generally agree that the wrists are not to be trusted with the delicate determination of the length you wish to hit the putt at hand. Though of tremendous importance in wood and fairway iron shots, the wrists become an untrustworthy medium when it comes to putting. They're too variable!

Implicit in putting technique is the intent to take as much play—meaning turning or twisting of the wrists or body—out of the putt as possible. More putts are missed by poor stroking than poor judgment of line or distance. Any improvement you can make to eliminate faults of deviation or side swing will guarantee you better greens results.

METHODS TO INSURE GOOD GRIP AND STANCE

Now let's discuss the steps in taking a good grip and a good stance when putting, and later take up the matter of lining up putts, reading greens, judging slopes and rolls, and so on.

The surest way to keep a putting stroke true is to keep the hands square against each other. That may sound easy, yet it requires concentration and constant checking, not only at the outset but all the while you play golf. Once you have acquired good habits, they should become automatic, but you will find even then that an occasional corrective check is necessary.

In taking the grip, be certain you take one which will insure complete uniformity of action of both hands. The grip could be the reverse overlap such as I use, or any of a number of others, including the overlap or even the interlocking grip used on fairway irons.

Some fine putters merely put the first two fingers (index and second finger) of the left hand up and over the back fingers of the right, not tightly but just enough to have a firm hold on the club. I do not recommend it, but I have seen it used effectively.

There is one hard-and-fast rule which is important in regard to putting. The tighter you grip the club, the less distance you will hit the ball. You will discover this with a bit of experimentation.

For most people the left thumb should be straight down the shaft in a natural position, and firmly imbedded in the haft of the right palm.

The right thumb can be placed in a variety of positions, but guard against triggering it or against any other position which would give it too much importance in holding the club (see Fig. 52). Generally speaking, the soundest and least dangerous position for the right thumb is also down the shaft, but never tense or tight.

There is considerable argument among putters as to whether the left or the right hand should be the motivating force in starting the putter back. I believe that the left hand can initiate the action, but also am convinced that the right hand should be in stronger control of the grip at all times.

This is something which you must work out yourself since the nuance of good control rests in your own hands, so to speak. Always bear in mind the fact that the hands should be in parallel opposition as to grip, and in complete unison during the swing.

The putting stance is different from that taken on any other shot you might hit. For one thing it is lighter, narrower, and easier, since very little force of impact is required. For another, you are standing more over the ball because of the straighter shafting of the putter, and much more in a crouch. Nor do you have the problem of violent weight shift through the successive stages of muscular action that is required of a tee or fairway shot.

I advocate the braced left leg, which you putt against, but I have not made that a hard and fast rule of putting. But if you do set the left foot and leg firmly, it should remain in that position throughout the swing. Any tendency to sway is bound to affect your aim.

The muscles as a power source should be kept out of the putting swing as much as possible. I know good putters who have a circular motion of the head of the putter on their swing, which indicates some action of the arms. But they are so few and their margin of error is so precarious that I would warn any but the most adept to guard against developing such action.

The touring pros, ever ready to try anything which might help their putting even a little bit, have tried and universally discarded any tendency to use the wrists in putting. They have found by experiment that there is little or no chance of obtaining uniformity of action from one putt to the next when the wrists are mobile.

One of the outstanding veterans of pro golf and one the finest teachers today strongly advocates the stiff left wrist on every shot, but particularly in putting. I agree wholeheartedly because I do not believe anyone can flex the wrist exactly the same way each time.

TENSION. With the left leg braced and the right leg a sort of prop or brace, there is a tendency to tense up when putting. By all means eliminate this tension.

A majority of good putters have found that a slight flex or bending forward of the knees will help to relieve this tension, which is inclined to develop particularly at the crucial point of address. Also, players inclined to nervousness sometimes have a difficult time starting the clubhead back. That is mental.

As I said before, the face of the putter should always be exactly square to the line you intend to hit the ball. I call particular attention to "the line you intend to hit the ball," since many have the impression that the center of the face of the club should always be set square to the hole, regardless of the line of roll of the putt.

When your reading of the green indicates a "borrow," or a curving roll around or across a slope, you mentally move the cup the foot, yard, or whatever distance to the right or left which you have figured as the proper path. Although this takes some doing, some development of the imagination, it is absolutely necessary.

If you use this method, which I have found most effective on tricky side-hillers, then your club face must be square to the imaginary position of the cup. Your action during address and look-see should be to the point you have chosen as the zenith of your arc of putting, not to the hole itself.

Your upper torso, head, and shoulders should not be rigid as you prepare to stroke the ball, just firmly anchored. I would say the only movement they should make is a slight lateral shift, and then mainly on the longer putts.

Any pointing or turning of the shoulders in the course of the swing might produce off-line or less-than-square-face hitting of the ball. This is difficult to explain on paper, yet easily demonstrated. Bear in mind that everything you do while putting should concentrate on rolling the ball down the exact line you have selected (or "read," as they say of a putt) with relaxed firmness.

The crucial point of putting is the moment of starting the club back after address and sighting. The club must be brought back on a low plane closely parallel to the ground and very little above it, yet enough above so that there is no danger of stubbing the clubhead.

A golfer whom I regard as one of the best putters in the business says the crux of the putt is in the first five inches of the backswing. He means that the initial path and plane the clubhead takes as the club starts back will be the determining factor in the entire route of the club both backward and forward. If you don't start the clubhead right, the entire shot can be ruined, since there is no margin for correction during the brief movement of the clubhead.

HITTING TECHNIQUES

At this point I would like to give my pupils a choice of several techniques of hitting the ball. Try them out and select the method which seems most efficient.

Those with the "gift," so to speak, prefer an easy, gentle sweep through the ball. Never, but never, neglect to examine the lie and line before taking address. Perhaps a great deal of a good putter's mastery is inherent, but don't forget the endless hours these masters have spent perfecting their silk-smooth technique.

Although it might not seem so, the sweep or brush technique is the most difficult stroke of all, because it requires so much more control. This holds true particularly on short putts where there is an almost irresistible temptation to overswing.

No part of any golf swing can be perfected without a lot of practice, and I believe sweep putting requires as much time to learn as any phase of the game. Remember this when choosing your method.

Another distinct way of contact with the ball is the so-called tap putt. Actually this is a mild jab at the ball with little or no follow-through.

In developing this type of hitting, guard religiously against any nudging or nipping on the stroke. The tap putt should have just as much smoothness and unity of action of body and arms as the sweep.

One of the finest tap putters in the game probably would be a fine putter if he used the sweep style, but he thinks the tap gives him a little edge because it does not require as much technique. Also advocates of the tap putt claim it has a little more roll that the sweep at the end and sometimes nips the cup where the sweep will stop short. Certainly the good tapper drops an unusual number of putts which nudge up to the hole, either dead center or on either side, and seem to collapse into the cup instead of hanging on the edge. But on second thought, so do the good ones using other techniques.

You should have the feeling of striking a downward blow on the putt, almost as if the face of the putter were tilted toward the hole, with the top edge nearer than the bottom. But that is only a feeling. I don't believe this tilt is possible to do in a normal stroke unless the player consciously exaggerates the stroke by keeping his hands far ahead of the clubhead, a difficult and disastrous maneuver at any time.

Actually when you have this feeling, you will guarantee getting the clubface squarely into the ball at contact, the ultimate objective in putting.

ADDRESS

The putt should be addressed a wee bit ahead of the center of an imaginary line you might draw at a right angle to the line of the toes on address when you use the left-side brace. If you prefer the balanced stance, then the putt is addressed dead center of the body.

In both cases the exact center of the face of the club is where you must hit the ball, not ever from out on the toe or back on the heel.

Make sure you do not ever address the ball in such a way that you will be forced to reach out for it as you come through to impact.

In a good address the arms and hands should be close to, but not touching, the body, with the knees slightly bent, as I mentioned before. Also make sure that there is no body rigidity.

Never take a stance which cramps the body, arms, or legs or that is out of line. I have seen club golfers try to putt from an open stance, with which they have no chance of keeping a true line. And the same applies to using the closed stance, in which the left foot is out ahead of the right. This fault guarantees a natural block of action.

I find that I get better results, and a better aim at the cup, if I place the face of my putter in the exact position I want to hit the ball *before* I take my stance. In effect, I let the position of the club face, held loosely in one hand (the left as a rule), determine the stance position I take when I step into my address.

THE SURVEY

Before I place the clubhead preparatory to taking my stance, I will have gone through an extremely important part of good putting—the survey. This is a department which the average golfer neglects woefully, yet the experienced professional considers it an invariable ritual on which his living mainly depends.

A careful survey of the green and the ground to be covered between

Fig. 53. First line up your putt from back of the ball.

the ball and the cup is about as necessary as having a ball to play the game. I am aware that sometimes it appears tedious and unnecessary to the spectator at a championship. Believe me, it is far from that.

The mental analysis of all the putting factors involved—speed of the green, hidden rolls, amount of impetus to be imparted, etc.—is by no means all there is to it. The good golfers realize also that they are about to adjust

Fig. 54. Give it a look from the side. Perhaps there is a roll which you did not see. And also take a look from the hole to the ball to verify your previous observations.

themselves from one physical action to another. To reach the green, they have had to swing hard and free with some violence for the drive, fairway shot, and perhaps an approach pitch.

Fig. 55. You are ready for the shot that can save more strokes than 300-yard drives in the course of one 18-hole round.

Now they must discard this type of action and hit a controlled short shot with complete composure. The survey of the green offers the bit of time necessary to make this change of pace.

Every putt outside of the five- or six-inch "gimme" should be lined up

Fig. 56. Just as figured from careful observation before taking the stance, the ball rolls a bit left as it comes to the cup. It did—and dropped!

at least three ways: from the front (back of the ball looking at the cup), from the back (beyond the cup looking from it to the ball), and from either side. In the case of a sidehill roll or an intervening mound, it might be well to look at the putt from both sides.

Fig. 57. Always give the flag a chance to help you in a putting survey by using its perpendicular angle as an added check point.

During this examination, the experienced golfer also will be checking the grass and grain of the green, the mowing, the wind, the moisture, and all the other things which determine the speed of the green. In other words, the player is judging in his mind the exact amount of impulse which must be imparted to get the ball to the cup. A good putt should always be strong enough to go by the cup if it doesn't drop. "Never up, never in" can be the saddest words in golf.

Most people have a difficult time reading the "grain" of a green, meaning the way the grass is lying. My method, and that of my contemporaries, is to determine the grain during my examination of the lie from in back of the ball.

If the grass shines from the glint of the sun, or even without it, you know that the grain runs away from the ball to the cup. That means your putt will run a bit faster than against the grain. By examining the putting line from in back of the cup, you have a good check on this.

Grain is more important to the average golfer than to the championship contenders because of course upkeep procedure. Normally clubs will abstain from cutting the greens too closely until a big tournament, which means that the surface is much slower, and the graininess emphasized. Close-cut greens have far less grain.

The matter of side slopes must be considered, too. When the grain is against you, the ball will not borrow quite as much because the tips of grass are inclined to slow down the roll and the turning of the ball.

I mentioned previously that the firmer you grip the putter, the less length you will get. Now I give you a place to use that firmer grip—on putts going downhill. Here you can use the added braking which comes automatically with a tightened grip.

Conversely, the uphill putt must be loose, but not weak. Here you try to get the feeling of the ball dropping into the cup and avoid any tendency to steer. Of all the putts you may have, the downhill putt with a curl will always be the most difficult, not merely to size up but also to keep your body from trying to add a little something extra to the stroking for compensation.

MISCELLANY

The tour pros will vary the weight of their putters according to the turf of the course they are playing. A majority carry at least two putters with them, and usually more, to make a choice when they come to a course which has different greens.

The stars also will go from a blade putter to a mallet if their greens play goes sour. The blade, lighter and a bit more delicate of touch, is best for fast greens, while the mallet is considered the superior weapon when the greens are heavy and slow.

The shafting of a putter is not considered as important as in the long-hitting clubs, and top players generally will go along with the shaft put in by the manufacturer.

Some prefer to have a wooden shaft, believing it gives a better feel to the putt. However, wooden shafts are easily affected by weather, and are apt to bend or bow if not properly stored. Perhaps someone should invent a press for wooden shafts in between use such as they use to keep tennis racquets in true.

It is estimated that 80 per cent of putts are missed on the left side, which has been nicknamed the "amateur" or "sucker" side. This fault stems from a tendency to turn the face of the club in at impact.

When you find yourself continually missing to the left, do something about it. Straighten out the face of the club. But never attempt to aim more to the right to compensate for the slight turning-in of the clubface. This never can be a constant method of stroking and should be eliminated rather than adjusted by a different stance facing.

A great many golfers prefer to put the index finger of the right hand down the club shaft, and I have seen some pretty good efforts with this style. However, I would not recommend it under any circumstance.

For one thing, it puts too much control in that single finger. It also restricts the muscles of the right hand by cramping them. I don't believe that muscle is necessary in good putting, but I fail to see how any advantage can be gained by straining the muscles and tendons of one hand with an abnormal grip.

Stick to your own style of putting, once you have decided which is your most effective one. Don't be swayed by the magic putting of some playing partner into imitating or adopting his style. A golfer who tries to copy the technique of the last good putter he watched will never master the art.

He is a bit like a trick-shot star I know who frequently tried tournament golf, then complained that when it came to making a crucial shot, he could usually think of three different ways of hitting the ball. Invariably, in a case like this, whichever way the trickster selected was always the wrong one, not because he stroked poorly, but because he never was quite certain he had chosen the correct way.

Above all, learn to stroke slowly on every putt, after making certain you have the complete picture of length, roll, and target. Practice the slow motion until it is automatic. Putting isn't easy, either to learn or maintain. But it is wonderfully rewarding when you find the touch.

8

Help for the
Average Golfer

With the exception of the part devoted to putting instruction, my golfing counsel thus far has been devoted to basic principles aimed principally at teaching the beginner the proper fundamentals of the golf swing—grip and stance, arm and body action.

The beginner, of course, should be grounded on the basics leading to the development of a sound swing. The player who really needs help in the way of correction and review is the average player, meaning the club golfer who is the backbone of the game.

The need for correction and review applies to top players, too, since their swings go out of kilter all too frequently with imperceptible kinks which creep in all too easily. The professionals and low-handicap amateurs who practice frequently generally have a better understanding of the principles of good play and therefore are better equipped to make their own adjustments when the swing goes awry.

The average club player lacks the time, background, and complete comprehension of the elements of a good swing for such self-study. So when his game goes sour, he definitely is in trouble. He thus needs expert outside advice and systemized instruction.

Perhaps there is the question of what grade of performance describes an average club golfer. To me, he is a fellow, or a lass, who has played the game for some time, anywhere from a year to ten years. He or she possesses some ability to hit the ball, frequently coming up with really good shots.

Scoring may range from 80 up to 100, with a handicap of anywhere from 8 to 24. In many cases the average golfer will run the full range of these scoring extremes from day to day. I will say that any of these players, were they able to take a few weeks just to play in between intensive drill sessions and with no other diversions, would not only develop a scoring potential well below their handicap norm but would also find themselves playing much more consistently.

BRINGING YOUR SCORE DOWN

The player who can occasionally break 80 is within range of staying regularly under 75. The club golfer who shoots in the middle 80's likewise has a far greater potential than he realizes. Believe me, very few club players do themselves justice on the course, not merely with their swing but also from the standpoint of good golf thinking.

I can cite one illustration which will bring this point home to every golfer. Supposing you, a middle-80 player, should go out several times in succession with three other fellows who are much better players—say, around one or two handicap. The higher-handicap player will play and score much better without any conscious volition because he will have greater incentive and more concentration.

Better golf is inherent in every golfer, and I go right on through to include our greatest champions in this statement. The better players may not have as much need for improvement, but conversely they will work harder to correct a minor fault than the club golfer will to correct a major one, such as a tendency to shank, if you will pardon the word.

CHECK POINTS IMPORTANT. The good golfer has some ability to analyze and review his swing from start to finish. He has several check points which he can use as indications of any variation from his norm.

The more perceptive ones do not always wait until their swing comes apart completely to go through routine checks. The smart players develop a habit of running through the various crucial spots of the swing at frequent

Fig. 58. A check point on any tee or fairway effort. The left knee should be pointing out beyond the ball at the top of the swing.

intervals, starting with the grip, continuing with stance, tempo of the swing, and so on all the way. This readily shows how precarious good form can be.

It does not require any deep inside knowledge of golf to set up such check-point procedure. Certain fault points can quickly determine whether the swing is in groove or has latently developed some quirk which can be costly, strokewise and betwise.

I have dwelled on this phase of play at some length because I would like my pupils to install the quick review as a part of their over-all approach to the game. If they will learn to take a good look at certain parts of their action ever so often, they are bound to build a sounder and less variable technique.

GRIP IS EASY TO CHECK. Just for instance, let's consider the grip. Here there is always the visual check point of the V's between the thumb and forefinger of each hand (see Fig. 59). If these V's point approximately over the junction of the neck and right shoulder (some say to the right eye, others to the right shoulder tip, and either could be right), then the placement of the hands is fairly normal.

If one of the hands is so placed that the V does not point upward to this area, correction is in order. This is probably the easiest check in the entire swing.

Because this is so, it would seem almost impossible for the grip to get out of whack. Yet it will, time and again, even among the top tour stars. There is a tendency to let the right hand turn just a bit under, leaning toward the baseball grip—probably because it lends a false sense of getting

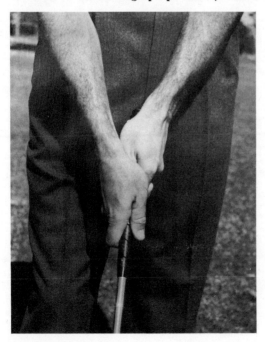

Fig. 59.   Are your V's in line?

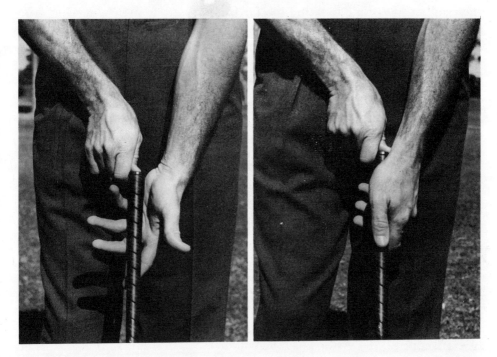

Fig. 60.   Watch that placement of the left hand on the club, putting it at least
an inch below the haft (end) of the club.

greater power. When this happens the left hand also is apt to turn on
over as well, cramping it and giving the right hand far too much control,
which is a perfect way to bring about a lot of ducking hooks (see Fig. 60).

With some, I have noticed an opposite reaction of the left hand. This
hand will also turn under to compensate for the turning under of the
right hand. This fault will completely ruin timing, smooth swing action,
and clubhead speed at impact.

A faulty grip does more than get the club and swing out of its grooved
path. It also tends to interfere with the proper application of power—the
gradual acceleration which explodes exactly at impact.

Instead, the average player is apt to apply his greatest effort at the top
of the swing, or as it starts downward. By the time the clubhead gets to
the ball it has lost much of its force. This, of course, brings on that big,
awful slice which is the bane of most golfers. Any forcing of action with
the hands gets them "ahead" of the swing, so much so that it is impossible
for the wrists to break the club into the square hitting position at impact.

HOW TO CORRECT A SLICE

If you find yourself baffled with the slice, and unable to get out of it,
here is a simple trial-and-error procedure to try on the practice tee. Since

most golfers are prone to swing too far back, try a few swings in which you radically cut down your backswing to the height of the hips.

Hit some balls from there, then start going back a little and hit away. I dare say you will be surprised at both the distance you will get hitting the ball from about shoulder height, and how much straighter the ball will fly.

Forget about such general terms as a "firm left side," "straight left arm," and other phrases which are meaningless unless applied with full understanding of the mechanics of the swing.

For instance, you will hear a golfer say he "is blocking." If he knows what it means, it indicates that he is not coming through easily and smoothly because he is keeping his left side and arm unusually rigid.

The stars use this technique to achieve certain results at crucial moments. I saw a championship clinched with a firmly set, unyielding left wrist as the player hit a long No. 4 iron to the final, and winning, green. The new champion was in a tight spot where a stray ball could ruin his chance of victory, with a strong breeze blowing across the elevated green from right to left.

By blocking that wrist firmly, thus giving the left hand and arm a bit of extra control, the victor knew he could not possibly hook the ball. The way the wind was blowing and the alarming variety of trouble lurking all down the left side of the hole demanded that he force a left-to-right trajectory.

But the average club golfer cannot indulge in such advanced techniques. Let him block his left side and his entire swing would go far out of kilter.

PRACTICE WITH A PURPOSE

The point I made above, about experimenting with the length of the backswing on the practice tee, brings to mind the average player's lack of practice knack. Outside of a brief warm-up before teeing off for any round, a session of hitting balls aimlessly is mainly wasted time.

Every time you go out to hit a bag of balls it should be for a definite purpose. I just don't mean a lot of experimentation, since that leads nowhere unless there is a specific target for improvement. First check the things I enumerated a few paragraphs back—grip, stance, swing tempo. Make sure, for instance, you have not unconsciously crept back on the ball, meaning that you are playing it too far off the left of the middle.

Now get down to facts. What club did you hit poorly most often in your previous round? Ask yourself why. What was the worst feature— a big slice, topped ball, weak hitting, erratic chipping, or whatever? What was the reason for it?

Those are some key questions which can lead to constructive effort. If you are unable to think of any practice action which will tend to overcome the erratic behavior of your ball, then consult your professional, which is never a bad idea when you are in a quandary anyway.

KNEES CAN TELL A STORY

I have mentioned several check points in the swing, but I have not mentioned the knees, since they are a bit more advanced in the progress of a golfer's development.

At the top of the backswing, your right knee should be bent and pointing behind the ball. Your left knee should be bent and slightly down. If your leg action does not conform to this general formula, then try to swing so that it will.

Never try to correct one fault by exaggerating another. The swing cannot stand any deviating corrections. Once set in motion, the swing is a chain reaction, and it will stay out of whack if it is not started properly.

The best way to avoid bad swing habits is to work on good ones, always pursuing a course which will develop smoothness and timing.

Your swing will undergo some subtle changes from time to time. That is inevitable. As many experts have said, you cannot go one way all the time.

But don't let this change creep in unconsciously. Recently I found myself hitting more and more hooks and knew I had to do some reviewing. I found that I had drifted into a more open stance than was necessary, but did not realize it until I had gone the gamut from check point to check point.

I was compensating by keeping my hips more closed. That is bound to cause body contortion on the swing and loss of control. The most likely development in such a case is the loss of good hip action, which brings on swinging with the shoulders.

THE VALUE OF CONCENTRATION

The average golfer, I can say flatly, lacks the ability to concentrate, which probably is the most important component of any good game. I believe the ability to concentrate is the difference in skill between the club player and the golf professional, even more than shot-making prowess.

Concentration is not easily mastered, to be sure. I would say it takes more "practice," if that is the word, than any other phase of the game.

The question often is asked what a golfer should think of while hitting the ball. The answer is "nothing."

All the thinking-out of any shot—distance, arc, direction, technique—

should be accomplished before the clubhead starts back. Mull over all factors pertaining to a particular shot before the stroke is started back. From there on the mind should be a blank, letting the body take over the full swing mechanics.

I have heard people jeer at a golfer who becomes disturbed over the clicking of a camera, the jingle of pocket coins, a sudden shout or yell, or the movement of a nearby foot within eye-range when he starts the club back. Yet I know this is no mere resentful reaction of an over-nervous psycho.

Actually the unexpected interruption breaks the affected player's concentration on pure blankness. He is listening unwillingly, and his mind is thus diverted from the pure physical effort he is making, and his timing goes blooey. It is wonderful if you can remain oblivious to outside noises, but it is rarely possible.

STANCE IS NOT A METHOD

Earlier in this book I listed the various types of foot placement—the hook stance (left foot advanced beyond the right), slicing stance (right foot ahead of the left), and the square stance.

The average golfer will do well to bear in mind that these are terms, and not guaranteed techniques to produce a hook, a slice, or a straight ball. In fact, the top players manipulate the ball with arms and hands, not the feet, although they will use foot placements in conjunction with their manipulation.

The average golfer would do well to avoid any such pedal maneuvering except as a potential corrective measure, and then only to try to develop straightaway shots. Any good golfer will tell you that the most difficult shot of all to hit consistently is the straight, undeviating ball down the middle. So if you can develop fairway hitting with some regularity, you are on your way to becoming a fine player.

THE TENDENCY TO UNDERCLUB

One of the principal shortcomings in the club golfer's game is his lack of knowledge of the distances of the club facings he uses. Time and again I see a high-handicap player haul out a club without any definite concept of the shot which he is about to make.

This may be due in part to lack of judgment of the distance, yet I have found mostly that the player has failed to calibrate the distances of his clubs properly. Distances vary slightly with every man, I might say, and with every different make of club.

The tendency is to underclub by selecting too short a club for the distance to be covered. Golfers, always eternal optimists, are apt to visualize

Fig. 61. Perfect rehearsal! Starting the backswing of a No. 5 iron in the practice area, the concentration should be even greater than in competition—to be sure of hitting it right.

their next shot as the equal of the best one they ever hit with that same weapon. It is much better to temper high expectancy with a bit of realism, and hit the club you know from experience will do the job.

Distance absolutes with each club may not be the full answer. Just for

Fig. 62. It is going to be a good shot. Three-quarters of the way up the body
is in good alignment, the arm and knee action unified.

instance, even if an average golfer determines that he can get, let us say,
ten yards more off the tee with a driver than he can with a brassie, I still
say he should use the brassie.

On long shots, accuracy-plus-distance is more important than sheer dis-

Fig. 63.   Almost at the top. The knee is on a fine point, the head position
excellent, and the hips have pivoted easily to full turn.

tance and no control. The tour professionals will frequently go to the
brassie, or even the spoon, when they find they are in one of those in-
explicable periods when they lose some control of tee shots. And believe
me, all of us suffer these unhappy moments.

Fig. 64. The top—and the pause. Now the body comes out of its backward coiling to start the downswing.

In the 1960 United States Open at Cherry Hills, the leading contenders used drivers on not more than five or six of the fourteen par 4 holes. Narrowed fairways, a premium on good placement for the second shot, and in many cases the short yardage of such holes as the 324-yard downhill first

Fig. 65. There never is any need to hurry a swing—or the weight shift. Note the strong left arm, maintained throughout the shot—a guarantee of good results.

made accuracy a necessity and pure distance too much of a gamble.

While on the subject of woods, I also want to note that the average player often errs in his choice between the No. 3 (spoon) and No. 4 woods. The more loft to the face, the less margin of off-line error for the player.

Fig. 66. The power zone! From here to the ball the hands add the clubhead speed which gets distance as the hips come around and the left side prepares to take the weight shift.

Therefore the No. 4 wood must be considered the safest of the four regulation clubs in any fairway lie.

If there is any question of the ball sitting badly, go to the No. 4 wood.

Fig. 67.   Certainly it was a fine shot! The position at the finish indicates smooth
action throughout.

If the ball lies in the rough but is playable for distance, always take the
No. 4 wood if you are determined to go for big yardage.

Bear in mind that a well-hit ball out of heavier grass whether with wood
or iron, will "fly," as the term has it, meaning that it will have an extra

Fig. 68.   Regular address to hit a No. 3 wood from the fairway.

amount of scaling flight because of the slide it gets off the clubface, most often because of grass or weed juice.

By the same token, it is wise to use one less loft of an iron in the same circumstance because of this overflight. I must add at this point that this extra-distance factor coming out of heavy grass (it also applies to uncut or wet fairways as well as short rough), cannot ever be a constant; it varies from one shot to the next. It is one shot which calls for caution and temporizing and definite underclubbing. The ball usually will have considerably more roll than usual, too, after it hits the ground.

9

Improving Your Iron Play

And so, let's turn to the use of the irons and approaching clubs by the average golfer. Here a mental chart of the distance you get with the various numbered clubs is far more important than with the woods. The difference in facing slope means something between ten and fifteen yards per club.

It can be a closer margin than this with the pitching clubs—Nos. 8, 9, and the wedges. But in these latter clubs, much more variable technique is permissible, depending on the length of the shot, its type (pure pitch-and-stop, or pitch-and-run), the terrain to be covered, the kind of green, the position of the pin itself, and so on.

I repeat that the average golfer is inclined to underclub by overestimating his own ability to hit the ball. In a majority of lessons at Tequesta Country Club, for instance, I find my pupils usually aiming to drop the ball on the front of the green with a short, let us say 40-yard, No. 9 iron pitch or with a wedge.

That is too short of the target with such a club. The absolute target on such a shot should be the feeling of trying to drop the ball right down the flagstick; in effect, trying to hole out on the fly. This is tempered only when the surface of the green in back of the pin slopes sharply down toward the player, which would force a dangerous putt. In such case, the up-tilted green will help stop the ball, generally eliminating the necessity to try the safer but much more delicate pitch-and-run.

This holds unless you have developed more proficiency with the pitch-and-run than with the pitch-and-stop. In every case where there is some doubt as to the better way to hit the ball, never hesitate for a moment to use the one you know you play best.

However, let us examine the irons in their order of numbering, from the long-hitting clubs down to the pitching irons.

THE NOS. 1, 2, AND 3 IRONS

I start with the No. 1 iron with some misgiving, since it is the one club which no beginner ever should try to swing without preliminary practice with other clubs. The No. 1, or driving iron, is nearly straight-faced and a distance club pure and simple. It is only for the expert who needs length but is saddled with the kind of a lie which precludes hitting a wood.

If a player is confident he can hit a No. 1 iron without forcing it (the key mental status for hitting all irons, but doubly emphasized here), then he has a better chance of getting the ball away.

Perhaps the No. 1 iron's greatest utility is when you must hit a boring shot into or across a stiffish wind. The ball can be kept under control and will ride into the breeze much better off an iron face than off a wood.

Don't ever grab the No. 1 iron until you have a good working idea of hitting all the other irons in the bag. In fact, not too many players, even among the touring troupe, carry a No. 1 in their kits. They prefer to substitute an extra wedge for the troublesome short chip shots which occur so much more frequently in a normal round.

For pure distance the No. 1 iron with its straighter, less-lofted face is bound to get you more yardage. But, believe me, you had better know how to hit it well. Nothing in golf can go as awry as a poorly struck driving iron. In the case of a whiff you have an advantage, at least, since you still have the same lie as before you took your cut.

For that matter, neither is the No. 2 iron a club to fool with at the very outset. It, too, is a distance-getter and requires a lot of practice and know-how to obtain consistent results.

With both of these straight-faced clubs, I would counsel a slightly longer backswing than with the shorter clubs. I cannot tell you how much longer, except not very much. That is something you must find out and work out for yourself.

Actually the No. 2 iron should be hit just about as you would hit your No. 4 or No. 5 iron, though perhaps played a wee bit ahead of the center line between the heels—not as much as might be taken with the driver but still in a strong hitting position for a strong club. The stance is fairly wide, too.

The maximum range of the No. 2 iron is about 200 yards if well struck. (I will give a table of average distances for the various irons at the end of this chapter on the irons. It is no absolute but merely a standard on which to base your own expectations.)

As you move down to the No. 3 iron, you are getting to the clubs which give you more visible loft and therefore a bit more confidence. The No. 3 still is a powerful weapon requiring considerable skill and firmness, but it will get you some height and a more controlled flight.

Many teachers advocate a variation of stance when using the long irons. They hold that it is advantageous to go to a bit more open position (left toe behind the line of the right toe with body slightly turned to face the line of flight). This can be overdone very easily. As far as I am concerned,

Fig. 69.   The No. 2 iron, played a bit forward of center, square stance and a
bit wider.

I would not advise it, yet I am not certain it should be completely taboo.

A major fault of many in using the No. 3, as well as the Nos. 1 and 2, is failure to stand a bit farther away from the ball. The shaft is longer and the swing fuller than with the medium irons. In standard clubs if the

Fig. 70.   The backswing with a No. 2 iron should be strong but not tense.

bottom of the face of the club is allowed to lie flat on the turf in back of the ball, the shaft will indicate the correct position to take a proper stance. Even the slightest cramping when hitting a No. 3 is apt to be disastrous.

The first trio of irons I have listed will always get a long roll after hitting the ground, except under unusual circumstances such as a soaking wet

Fig. 71. The follow-through duplicates in many ways the action of the club on the downswing.

course. I would also add sand to this and (mainly for future consideration as you progress) some special actions which the player might take to control that roll. However, this last-named category involves the use of advanced techniques and should not even be contemplated by the novice.

Fig. 72. A check point. Lay out a rough graph with two clubs and spot the ball. Take a natural stance with the No. 3 iron and see if your measuring conforms.

First learn to swing the club in a standard pattern, until you can hit the same shot time after time. I would even say that this might be the best motto to stick to and never ever think of special techniques.

THE NOS. 4, 5, AND 6 IRONS

The No. 4 iron, with a range up to about 170 yards, is a club with a feel which still will get good distance. In every iron shot the feeling should be of hitting down and into the ball. This perhaps becomes more noticeable with the No. 4. If you don't take a divot on an iron shot, you have not hit it well. But that doesn't mean tearing up the course by any means. And don't ever forget to replace your divot!

The No. 5 iron, the time-proven mashie of wooden-shaft days, is the basic club in your bag, as I have previously said and now reiterate. If you are not able to handle this club for good distance and some accuracy, then you had better learn how. I think the No. 5 iron, with its good loft, is the key between long and short iron play. For one thing it is the club with which to address the ball exactly in the middle, meaning the line extending out between the position of the two heels.

I would say the No. 5 iron is the perfect practice club to get the feel of the longer irons. The No. 7, of course, can be a pretty handy weapon too. I might even recommend it as the second club for beginners to use, once they have acquired the rudiments of good iron play with their No. 5 iron.

The No. 6 iron is, to my way of thinking, a No. 5 iron with a broader face. It has more loft than the No. 5, of course, but it is the club you should use to get elevation in the 135-yard to 145-yard range. I believe, too, that the No. 6 iron, if properly manipulated, can bring the first intimation to the beginner of how to hit a stop shot.

As a check point for timing, the No. 6 iron is an excellent club to try out, using a deliberately slower swing than the one you may have been employing with the No. 5 iron. Try it, and see what sort of flight, how much distance, and how much action you get when the ball lands. You might get a panoramic view of your entire game with this one trial.

NO. 7 IRON

The No. 7 iron, good for shots from 125 yards to maybe 145, moves into the pitching phase of golf—a division which the average golfer approaches with some confusion but which becomes important in stroke-saving.

The major temptation when using the No. 7 iron is to try to get more distance than should be obtained with this club, thus losing the control which is the important feature of this lofted iron. I have seen average players get up to 150–155 yards with a No. 7 merely by playing it off the right toe which, in effect, is giving it the loft at impact of a No. 5 iron. Nothing could be more damaging to consistent iron play than to develop such a habit. You must set for yourself a consistent, uniform procedure with each iron to make certain you will (1) take advantage of the loft of the club you are using and (2) keep the club under control.

Remember this: The stance should never be a closed one from the No. 7 iron down, even when trying to cut left-hand corners. Unless you have thoroughly rehearsed the art of hitting an intentional hook (right to left) shot, be safe and play the shot straight away even if it means going wide of the target, which is of course the hole. Such strategy will save you many a stroke and many a pick-up, although it may be painful at the moment.

PICK OUT ONE CLUB TO USE ON PITCH-AND-RUN. The No. 7 iron has one other important use. It is the handiest club in your bag when you want to pitch-and-run from five to fifteen yards off the green. The average player would do well to select one single club for this type of shot and work on it diligently. By so doing he will get a feel and a finesse which cannot be acquired by trying a variety of clubs, such as a No. 5 iron for a short pitch, long run, or a No. 2 iron for what might be called an overlong putt.

My advice on the No. 7 iron should not necessarily be taken as the final word. Some players prefer the No. 6 iron for this shot, and with good right. But I believe the No. 7 iron, which you will find will be about fifty-fifty air flight and run, is safer and easier to master.

The terrain, type of grass and its degrees of cutting, and various other factors enter into the hitting ensemble as well. The technique of swinging on this shot is the same as hitting a long iron, but the club is not taken as far back.

There is no such thing as a half-hit shot, remember. There are half-shots and quarter-shots and grades in between, but it cannot be done by easing up or varying the arm action on the swing. No one can possibly develop such proficiency. The distance should be controlled by the distance the club is taken back. Any attempt to hit an easy shot without taking a normal swing will throw timing and smoothness completely out of whack, not alone on that shot but perhaps for an extended period.

The tendency of the average golfer to improvise is bound to cost him many shots on his score. Part of such variation may be due to fear—of the shot itself, of the terrain, of the dire possibilities should the shot go wrong. If control of distance is obtained by control of the backswing, there are not nearly as many things which can go wrong.

NO. 8 IRON

The No. 8 iron moves one into the pure pitching clubs. The No. 8 can be a handy weapon for the pitch-and-run, but takes some knowing. The No. 8 has a range of about 110 yards to around 130 yards. It has a lofted face that gives a high arc to the flight of the ball, and nowhere near the ground roll of a No. 7. I favor its use to its maximum distance but not for the "finesse" shots.

The No. 8 iron should be played from a slightly more open stance than is used with the longer irons, but not wide open. The feet should not be close together as you would use on a short wedge shot. The No. 8 iron swing is full and solid, with no variations from the way you would swing a No. 5 iron, but with less expectation of distance and roll.

The average golfer, picking up a No. 8 iron, is apt to regard its deeper face and slant as indicating a pitch shot, and thus be tempted to try to manipulate the club. If it does affect you that way, do not use it, at least not without some rehearsal and realization of just what the club can do. Actually, I could say the same about any of the irons in the bag, but this advice applies particularly to the No. 8.

Regard it mainly as a utility club, between the flying No. 7 and the near-wedge action of the No. 9.

NO. 9 IRON

The No. 9 iron should be the most important stroke-saving club in the average golfer's bag, aside from his putter. It is the club which will teach him how to pitch and, with patience on the practice grounds, how to stroke those soft half- and quarter-shots which mean so much in keeping scores to a minimum in and around the green.

The true flying distance of a No. 9 iron, stroked fully, ranges from about 90 to 115 yards. You might get more distance with it, perhaps by standing a bit more ahead of the ball (i.e., playing it from off the right toe), but don't ever try it. There is a margin of potential error there which is dangerous territory. In swinging a golf club, never depart from the orthodox method and you will automatically eliminate one perilous phase of error.

I would say that it is permissible to use a slightly open stance with the No. 9 iron, and to bring the feet nearer together on address. The action of the swing is exactly the same as with any other iron, but the result and the flight will be different. The No. 9 iron, with its deep pitch, flies the ball up instead of out.

Until the average golfer has fairly well mastered his ability to hit a straight, uniform, full flight with the No. 9 iron, it is advisable to abstain from any tricky half- or three-quarter shots. These types of shots take some knowing.

TWO WAYS TO HIT A SHORT NO. 9 IRON. For instance, there are two ways of hitting a short, controlled No. 9. One is the shortened backswing which I have emphasized time and again. The other is to choke up on the grip, moving the hands down the leather.

This latter technique can be an effective way of cutting down a No. 9 iron from, say, 100 yards to about 75 yards. But don't try to choke the grip and then hit a quarter-shot (i.e., taking the club back a quarter of the way). The combination is more than apt to ruin the swing completely. I would say not to try the choke grip until you can hit ten shots on the practice tee with good results on each one. Even one missed shot out of these ten indicates a weakness in this technique.

There is a strong temptation to try to steer short shots, usually manifested with body sway, or too much movement of the shoulders. Actually a No. 9 iron shot is made with the hands and arms but with no exaggeration or stiffness of the torso.

All iron shots should be hit on the descent of the club—down and through the ball—getting the hitting edge into the ground just before contact. This is more strikingly apparent with the No. 9 iron, and so is the action of the face loft in getting the ball in the air. You never, never need to help a No. 9 iron get the ball up. The pitch of the blade will take care of that, just as it does in a descending scale as you go up the gamut of irons.

CHIP-AND-RUN

There is a division of the short shots which cannot be completely covered while discussing clubs according to their yardage potential and that is the chip-and-run shot. This is the method of approach which is universal in England, where the aprons (the areas just out from the greens which are not closely cropped) are hairy and the greens unwatered and therefore never soft enough from irrigation to help the ball bite, as is the case on America's well-doused golf acres.

The chip-and-run, in general, is just about what it depicts in words—half-carry in the air, half-run along the surface. It usually is made with a No. 5 or No. 6 iron, taking a short backstroke to assure control. The length of the backswing on this shot should be the determining factor in the length the shot will be hit.

This is no shot to try to develop as a scoring weapon at the very outset of learning the game. Pay no attention to the advice of your fellow amateurs, and save your attempts to master this important shot until you have developed more confidence. You will find it comes easier then.

It is the easiest shot to miss in the entire swing gamut, I think, unless you except putts. And even the latter are more reliant on judgment and direction. The chip-and-run is one of golf's great refinements. It demands some feel for distance and considerable control of flight.

The chip-and-run can become an unstable item without proper conception, execution and analysis—and long, tedious practice. It requires certain specialized techniques which require experience as well as trained ability to make the swing perform as the player wills.

Fig. 73. Approach a wedge pitch with relaxation. This is not a club to grip tightly or hit nervously.

THE WEDGE

So we come to the wedge, golf's greatest stroke-saving invention of modern times—to the experienced player, that is. To the average golfer, the

Fig. 74. Easy action must keynote the important move of taking back the wedge, with no jerking or lifting.

wedge, with its wide-flanged undersole and deep pitch, is Dr. Jekyll and Mr. Hyde, and a lot more Hyde than Jekyll.

The pro stars play a stroke-saving tune with their pitching wedge (differing from the sand wedge), while the average player never knows what

Fig. 75. The club should go through on the wedge shot just as with the other
irons—but no higher than it went back.

is going to happen when he hauls out the same club for one of those short
pitches.

The major problem with the club golfer comes in swing execution, and
the almost irresistible temptation to soften the shot with a little extra

body action. This is manifested principally by failure to cock (break) the wrists, producing a stiff-armed effort which can bring misery and soaring scores.

The wedge has a range from 40 yards to 95 yards. It can be used from any distance ten yards and beyond, but only if the user has developed good technique as well as understanding of controlled swing action for the shorter distances. A wedge shot which is not crisply hit can be a horror.

The wedge shot, even more than the No. 9, should be struck from an open stance with the feet close together. The heels should not be more than ten inches apart at the most.

The weight should be on the left foot and leg at address and remain there throughout. The club should be taken back slightly outside, but not dragged, and slightly inside on the way down, an action which follows naturally. It is not a chop stroke, but as upright as you can make it without losing control.

There is a distinct tendency to take too little backswing on this shot on short-range hitting. Average golfers fail to consider that the deep face of the club hits the ball up rather than out, and such a flight cuts down distance considerably. Some teachers advocate that the bull's-eye of every wedge shot should be the top of the flag, but this can be overdone. Yet there is no question but that a majority of wedge shots end up too short of the cup.

Unless your swing action with the wedge is firm and crisp, with a break of the wrists even if you are taking the club back only knee high, there is a tendency to push or scrape the shot instead of lofting it. This can produce some weird results and absolutely ruin both direction and accuracy.

DON'T TRY FOR BACKSPIN AT FIRST. Forget about getting backspin, such as you might see some of the stars obtain. The ball will stop if you develop a sound technique, and there is absolutely no necessity to worry about drawing a ball until you have learned how to use the wedge with complete confidence.

The wedge shot must be played in slow tempo, without haste or extra effort beyond that important cocking action of the wrists at the top of the backswing. Of all the clubs in the bag, I would say the pitching wedge is the most difficult to master and the most difficult one to keep at peak efficiency. Experts are forever working on pitch shots, especially the wedge.

The wedge is so constructed, with its wide flange running back on the undersole from the hitting edge, that it cannot dig or bite if properly struck into the ball. Actually it is the safest club in the bag from the standpoint of construction. It only needs careful but forceful handling to mean the difference between an 85 and a 75, plus a little help from the putter.

Here is a table of the approximate distances which can be expected of each of the irons. In each case a range is indicated which need not be considered mandatory, by any means, but merely an average to give a pattern for using the clubs.

	Yards	
No. 2	190 to	210
No. 3	170 to	190
No. 4	160 to	175
No. 5	140 to	165
No. 6	140 to	155
No. 7	130 to	145
No. 8	115 to	130
No. 9	90 to	115
Wedge	40 to	95

10

The Art of Playing
Sand Traps

Most golfers have a distinct aversion to sand except when lying on the beach or mixing concrete.

When the average golfer flails his shot into a bunker, it works havoc with his poise. Except on rare occasions when strategy demands, not even the most expert players tempt fate by deliberately aiming at a trap, although the modern tour star seldom has trouble getting the ball out fairly close to the pin.

In fact, the greatest single improvement in golf technique during the last thirty years has been the tremendous upgrading of trap-shot accuracy, brought about principally by the development around 1930 of the sand wedge. With some rehearsal and an understanding of the mechanics of playing a wedge properly, there is no need to fear the occasional mishap of firing a ball into a trap.

Three-quarters of consistent performance from traps is confidence that it can be done. If you can convince yourself you will always lift the ball from the sand on the first try, you are on the way to improved scoring.

Recovering from traps is no mystic art. It merely requires a studied, ritualistic technique, firmly performed. Actually, the club used for this type of shot is more perfectly designed for its purpose than any other in your caddy bag. Used with intelligence, it performs its duty automatically.

The first objective of a shot from sand is to get the ball out. Never mind trying to hole out or lay it up close as you once saw Sam Snead do. Those close ones will come when you develop proficiency and confidence.

There is no better club for a trap shot than the sand wedge with its broad flange underneath, its greater weight, and the deep loft of its face. Properly swung, it can do nothing else but slide through the sand on the flange to fly the ball up on a sharp angle according to an inviolable law.

Never consider hitting any shot other than the semi-explosion. It is quite possible to chip out of a trap without churning up a lot of sand, but it is ten times as difficult as the easy blast. You will seldom, if ever, see a tour golfer chip the ball from a trap. He knows from experience the perilous margin of error involved in such an effort.

The grip for a wedge shot from sand is the same as with any other iron. Actually, this is the only point in your game where it can be said that you take two grips, one with the hands, the other with the feet. If this sounds facetious, it is nonetheless tremendously important to get planted well when in sand. Dig into a solid position by wiggling your feet until you feel you have a firm stance, even if the sand comes to the top of your shoes.

The feet are planted a bit wider in sand than for an approach wedge or No. 9 iron shot, possibly as wide as you would use with a No. 4 or No. 3 iron from the fairway. The stance must be open, with the right shoulder half-turned toward the hole. The body weight should give the feeling of being evenly distributed, although some players believe they get better results by emphasizing a firm left side. But on this particular point make your own decision after a session of trial and error in the practice bunker.

Because of the shorter shafting of the sand wedge, the position should be well over the ball on address, but never crowding it. If there is any feeling of being cramped, you are too close.

Be sure to study the texture of the sand before you take your stance, and try to prove it up by the feel of it as you dig in with both feet. There are infinite varieties of sands, from the soft, powdery type to hard gravel which will resist even the flange of the heavy wedge. If the sand is wet, it will give the ball considerably more impetus with the same physical effort.

In an ordinary recovery from sand, you should aim the front edge of the club at a point about two inches behind the ball and hit exactly at that point. Now you are ready to take the club back.

The club should never be dragged back, but picked up sharply and smartly. The wrists break early, and the backswing should go no higher than three-quarters, or about shoulder level. Going beyond this height will cost dearly in accuracy and efficiency.

The distance the ball will be hit is determined by two factors—the length of the backswing and the point your club hits into the sand behind the ball.

That is the key point of using the sand wedge. I would advise the average golfer to pick a spot just about two inches behind the ball as his striking point and never deviate from that distance. Develop this hitting spot as a habit. The ball should be played from the mid-line or even slightly ahead.

I can advise a good practice gimmick on the two-inch aiming space. Get out in a trap some day and draw a line with your finger two inches back of the ball. Hit enough shots at this target so that you can come down into the line with consistent accuracy.

Remember, of course, that this is only practice. When you are playing a regular round, it is against the rules to touch the sand with anything but the feet. Even striking sand on the backswing incurs a one-stroke penalty.

Fig. 76. Long shot from sand is addressed the same as long fairway shot, but club must not touch the sand. Stance and grip should be relaxed.

Fig. 77. Starting club back for long sand shot requires extra care and precision; less effort than fairway counterpart.

Fig. 78.   Top of swing is controlled since player must avoid digging into sand
at impact.

Fig. 79.   On downswing, full control must be kept, and weight must be shifted quickly.

Fig. 80. The ball is on its way with no sand flying. The secret of long iron from shallow bunker is solid contact without digging.

Fig. 81. Follow-through shows full control exerted throughout long iron shot from sand, emphasizing control throughout.

OTHER TRAP SHOTS

Everything I have said to this point concerns the short pitch from just off the green. You will meet up with other types of sand shots where the technique is different, such as the long recovery out of a fairway bunker.

In such a case you must develop the ability to hit the ball at about the same instant the club sole is coming in contact with the sand, using whatever iron you think will get you safely out with the maximum obtainable distance.

Let's say you have pushed your tee shot into a fairway trap some 175 yards from the green. The lie probably will be fairly good, since such traps are not the deep, slope-edged type. If the ball were on the fairway, you might pick a No. 4 iron for the shot. With a fairly good lie you can use the same club.

In this case you take a normal stance and hit the same type of No. 4 iron you would off the fairway. But you must be much more careful of the point of impact, bringing the clubhead in at the exact point of sand and ball.

Unless you have an unusually good lie, and no flaring bank of the hazard ahead of you, don't ever be tempted to try a wood from sand. It can be done, of course, but you are gambling against too heavy odds because of the pinpoint precision demanded of such a shot. It is much better to be almost to the green with a safe effort than to bloop a topped shot a few yards or, worse still, leave the ball in the bunker.

LOFT FOR CLEARING BANKS. While speaking of playing over the bank of a bunker, always make sure you take a club with enough loft to give the initial lift needed to raise the ball over the mound. There is nothing so disconcerting as a well-hit shot which doesn't get elevation quickly enough to carry the bank of the bunker.

On uphill and downhill lies frequently encountered in trap play, follow the same procedure you would with similar shots in the fairway. Play the ball a bit ahead on an uphill lie, a bit behind when it is downhill. You can overcome the disadvantage of hanging lies to some extent in traps by digging hard with the foot which takes position on the slope, even to obtaining a normal flat position if you wriggle in the foot firmly enough.

There is one other trap problem which occurs frequently—the ball which buries when coming in on the fly. Never let a buried ball scare you. Simply "hood" the club, turning the face in toward you, and fire away with normal vigor. The ball will come out surprisingly well. Here I would advise a session or two in a practice trap to convince yourself it works.

Fig. 82. Stay well over the ball when hitting an explosion from the trap preferably with wedge (or No. 9) and don't let the club touch the sand.

Fig. 83. A wedge is taken up sharply and abruptly and knees do not break too much. Position over ball must be maintained.

Fig. 84. Contact! The pitch of the wedge will assure lifting the ball out of trouble, and the front flange will automatically cause follow-through as it bites in.

Fig. 85.   Never leave a pitching club stuck in the sand.   Only a shot which has a complete follow-through will be effective.

Index

143